D0850002

Epochs of Economic Theory

Epochs of Economic Theory

A. K. DASGUPTA

Basil Blackwell

© A. K. Dasgupta 1985

First published 1985

Basil Blackwell Ltd
108 Cowley Road, Oxford OX4 1JF, UK

Basil Blackwell Inc.
432 Park Avenue South, Suite 1505,
New York, NY 10016, USA

British Library Cataloguing in Publication Data

Dasgupta, A. K.
    Epochs of economic theory.
    1. Economics
    I. Title
    330.1   HB171
    ISBN 0-631-13786-6

Library of Congress Cataloging in Publication Data

Dasgupta, A. K.
    Epochs of economic theory.
    Includes index.
    1. Economics–History.   I. Title.
    HB75.D263   1985   330'.09   85-1432
    ISBN 0-631-13786-6

Phototypeset by Dobbie Typesetting Service, Plymouth, Devon
Printed in Great Britain by The Camelot Press Ltd, Southampton

Contents

6 MARGINALIST CHALLENGE

7 A NEO-CLASSICAL SYNTHESIS: ALFRED MARSHALL

8 KEYNESIAN PERSPECTIVE

9 OVERVIEW

Preface

The following chapters grew out of an address which I presented to the Indian Economic Association at its Annual Conference in 1960.[1] In it I argued that the systems of economic theory, as they have grown over the years, have attempted to answer specific questions that assumed importance from time to time, and they are to be viewed as independent of each other. I argued, for example, that marginalist economics ('neo-classical', as it is often misleadingly called), far from being an emendation of classical political economy, was a challenge to it, having shifted economic theory away from the problem which concerned the classical economists. Similarly, modern growth theory, in so far as it is derived from Keynesian economics, I argued, was as far removed from marginalist economics as the latter was from classical political economy. The history of economic thought, I submitted, could be seen as consisting of 'epochs', each epoch giving rise to a new set of questions, and hence to new theories for answering them.

Friends advised, and I agreed, that the thesis deserved following up. I indeed promised myself that I would write a book illustrating my propositions by reference to the major shifts that have taken place in economic theory in the course of its development. The project, however, was held up for a long time; various assignments took me to other fields of research. It was only in 1976 when I accepted an invitation from Jawaharlal Nehru University to an honorary professorship that I regained my interest in the project. There were no specific duties attached to the job, and the atmosphere in the University was congenial to theoretical speculation. I gave a course of lectures to the University's School of International

---

[1]"Tendencies in Economic Theory', *Indian Economic Journal*, January–March, 1961; reproduced in my *Planning and Economic Growth* (George Allen & Unwin, London, 1965).

Studies during the sessions 1977–80, in which I presented an outline of my scheme. The response from those who attended was encouraging. A grant from the Indian Council of Social Science Research provided a further stimulus. Yet progress was slow, and I do not know how long I would have taken to finish the work had it not been for a persistent pressure from Amartya Sen and Partha Dasgupta, to whom I dedicate the book.

While the work was in progress I presented a summary view of the project in my C. N. Vakil Memorial Lecture held under the auspices of the Indian Economic Association in 1980.[2] Traces of this lecture will be noticed in the present book.

I should remind the reader that this is *not* a book on the history of economic theory. Its aim is rather to provide a perspective for viewing the history of economic theory. The development of economic theory is shown here, as was indeed done earlier, as consisting of epochs, each epoch being marked by specific historical and socio-economic situations. To illustrate my point of view I have chosen representative economists from each epoch, beginning with Adam Smith and concluding with John Maynard Keynes. Attention has been drawn in particular to the metamorphosis of capitalism and its impact upon economic theory over the period.

During the past few years I have had discussions on various aspects of my work with colleagues and friends. I have profited greatly from these discussions. My chief debt is of course to Amartya Sen and Partha Dasgupta, who not only encouraged me in my work from the outset but also made valuable comments on earlier drafts. There is also another name which I would gratefully mention. Marion O'Brien not only undertook to do the final copy for the Press, accepting the drudgery of inserting the author's corrections and emendations over months, she also wrote understanding notes to me on the chapters as she typed them. This was reassuring. The unenviable job of rescuing the text from a most clumsy manuscript fell on Shib Narayan Prasad, who did it cheerfully. Among those of my friends and colleagues who in the course of the progress of

---

[2]'How One May View the Development of Economic Theory', *Indian Economic Journal*, January–March, 1981; reproduced in my *Phases of Capitalism and Economic Theory* (Oxford University Press, Delhi, 1983).

the work stimulated my thinking, I would make special mention of Sabyasachi Bhattacharya, Sukhomoy Chakravarty, Sandwip Das, Amita Datta, Amlan Datta, Anupam Gupta, Ashok Mitra, Iswari Prasad and Samar Ranjan Sen. Finally, I am most grateful to René Olivieri for the intimate interest that he has shown in the publication of the book.

A. K. Dasgupta
Santiniketan
May 1985

To Amartya and Partha
but for whose encouragement
the book would not have been written

1
Preview

Relativity of Economic Theory

Historians of economic theory seem inclined to believe that there is a continuity in the development of their science. The progress of economic science is supposed to be continuous and cumulative in a manner in which the progress of sciences usually is – a progress from the particular to the general. If, it is contended, the labour theory of value has been supplanted by the marginal utility theory, it is because the latter provides a more general framework for the interpretation of value as it operates in the market, covering cases which the labour theory could not accommodate. Similarly the theory of underemployment equilibrium is said to be a more general theory, covering cases of market failures which the Walrasian system did not envisage; indeed the author of the theory overtly claims it to be a general theory, subsuming 'full employment' equilibrium as a special case.

It is my contention in this book that this manner of viewing the development of economic theory is misleading. It no doubt has an appeal to those who, like Joseph Schumpeter, would like to claim for economic science a status similar to that of the physical sciences. But the claim, it is contended here, is exaggerated; it ignores elements which distinguish economics conspicuously from the physical sciences. It is not the problem of precision, or lack of it, which concerns us here, for on this account the difference between the two sciences is one of degree only; propositions of economic science are admittedly less precise than those of the physical sciences, in so far as they are used to interpret reality. The difference that we would here emphasize is one of kind, a difference which arises from the fact that the propositions of economic science do not satisfy what one might call the universality criterion. The reality with which

1

the physical sciences are concerned is supposed to be given and constant. The assumptions that a scientist makes concerning the occurrence of physical phenomena are thus valid universally not only with respect to space but also with respect to time. The apple falls on the ground at all places and has done so, one imagines, at all times. New phenomena are no doubt discovered from time to time, which necessitate revision of existing theories. However, it is not that these phenomena did not exist before, it is only that they were not known before. The objective world is not supposed to change, it is the scientist's appreciation of it that changes. The scientist thus builds one theory upon another, so as to accommodate more phenomena than had been observed before. 'A scientist's present thoughts and actions', writes P. B. Medawar, 'are of necessity shaped by what others have done before him; they are the wave-front of a continuous secular process in which the past does not have a dignified independent existence of its own.'[1] The description does not fit economic science (or indeed any social science). Economists deal with a universe where data are freakish and are not valid universally, and where phenomena emerge which were not only not known before but had not existed before. It is of the nature of economic science that it involves events and phenomena which not only change complexion from time to time but do not also occur at all places. Problems that emerge as crucial at one time may turn out to be totally irrelevant at another time in the same economy, and those that are relevant in the context of one economy may well be irrelevant elsewhere. In economics old theories do not die. And they do not die not because one is built on the other but because one is independent of the other.

Consider, for example, the theory of wages. In the wake of the agrarian revolution in England a large body of labourers were released from the land; in view of the enclosure movement the former freeholders of land were deprived of their access to land, and mechanization of agriculture rendered the newly created landless labourers largely redundant. Industrialization, on the other hand, was yet in its early stage and altogether inadequate for the urban section to absorb the surplus labour. In such a situation, in so far as the labour market was free, a subsistence theory of wages could be vindicated as an approximation to reality. With the progress of industrialization, however, labour tended to become scarce, and

[1]P. B. Medawar, *The Hope of Progress* (Wildwood House, London, 1972), p. 105.

there had to be a substantial modification of the theory. Whereas previously the level of wages could be held as independent of demand, in the new situation demand came into its own and had to be reckoned as a determinant of wages. A theory which had a reasonable degree of validity in the context of the British economy in the early decades of the nineteenth century thus became totally irrelevant to the same economy by the second half of the century. Hence the emergence of what is known as the marginal productivity theory.[2] The advent of trade unions complicated the matter still further. The labour market took on the character of a bilateral monopoly where wage fixing came to depend on the relative bargaining power of the two parties, the employer and the employed. An element of indeterminacy was thus introduced in the labour market, calling for the intervention of the state. On the other hand, in a country like India, where the pace of industrialization and agricultural expansion is yet not commensurate with the growth of population, and where only a tiny fraction of the labour force is covered by trade unions, the older theory does seem to come closer to reality; a precarious physiological minimum sets the level of wages in such an economy.

The same sort of consideration applies to the theory of unemployment – to take another example, also from the labour market. How does it happen that an economy carries an excess supply of labour and yet remains in a state of equilibrium? This is the problem. The phenomenon may occur in an industrially mature economy, it may also occur in an underdeveloped economy. However, the explanation of the phenomenon is unlikely to be the same in the two cases. A theory of unemployment which is appropriate for one may not be so for the other. Thus the arrival of a new theory based on a possible 'insufficiency of effective demand' does not suggest demolition of an older theory which derives from a deficiency in the 'capacity of equipment'.[3] In economics, unlike in the physical

---

[2]Note that the marginal productivity theory of wages does not subsume the classical minimum subsistence theory. Where a minimum subsistence theory of wages applies, the marginal productivity theory fails. To know the marginal productivity of labour one has to know what the volume of employment is. However, in an economy where there is an abundance of labour, and where therefore wages are supposed to conform to the minimum subsistence of labour, employment is not given externally, and wages are determined independently of the demand for labour. It is, in fact, the marginal product of labour which in such cases adjusts itself to minimum subsistence.

[3]See M. Kalecki, 'Three Ways to Full Employment' in *The Economics of Full Employment* (Basil Blackwell, Oxford, 1945).

sciences, theories have grown laterally rather than in a hierarchical order. They are to be understood with reference to special contexts; to designate an economic theory as 'general' is somewhat over-ambitious.

It will perhaps be argued that our existing theories are yet incomplete, and that they may possess features which would lend themselves to further abstraction, thus providing possibilities of a hierarchical system. Such possibilities cannot of course be denied. Refinements of theories, so as to extend their explanatory domain, are as much a concern of economics as of the physical sciences. What is contended here, if our supposition concerning the occurrence of economic phenomena is correct, is that there are limits to such possibilities. As it is, the main developments in economic theory have taken place in specific historical contexts; herein indeed lies the distinctive property of economic science. Attempts to transcend them would seem to be a futile exercise.

Identification of Epochs

A system of economic theory evolves in response to questions that are provoked by a given set of circumstances in an economy. As circumstances change, or people's attitude to them changes, questions are revised, and a new system springs up. It is wrong to say that the new system is an improvement on an older one; it is different. No doubt there is often progress from a lower to a higher level of abstraction in a particular line of analysis. The passage from Smith's 'primitive' concept of division of labour to the modern theory of increasing returns is an outstanding example of such progress; one is derived from the other and is an improvement on the other. One would, however, go off on a false scent if one were to say this of the marginal utility theory as compared to the labour theory. These two theories, despite their appearances, belong to different planes of discourse.

In what follows the development of economic theory is seen as consisting of 'epochs'. Our frame of reference is the British economy. For it is there that the major innovations with which we are concerned took shape. Three epochs are identified – classical, marginalist and, as one would like to call it, Keynesian, from the name of the economist who ushered it in. It is contended that each epoch threw up specific questions, and economists devised modes of answering them.[4] Systems of economic theory grew out of these efforts. The systems, it is urged, should be viewed as independent of one another, answering different sorts of questions. The marginalist system does not mark a 'progress' over classical political economy, nor is it an alternative; it is different. The analytical technique that it offers, powerful as it is in the context of its own framework, is hardly relevant to the problems that are central to classical political economy. Nor does the Keynesian theory of aggregate output and employment have any direct affiliation with the marginalist theory of relative prices. No wonder that the author of the theory lumps Ricardian economics and marginalist economics together as 'classical' and dissociates his own economics from both.

The term 'epoch' is meant to stand for a 'period in history'. It does not, however, carry any suggestion of a revolutionary happening. Historians of economic theory often characterize the advent of marginalism as 'Jevonian revolution', or the advent of the theory of underemployment equilibrium as 'Keynesian revolution'. The characterization is misleading. The course of progress of economic science over the last two hundred years or so has not been smooth. There have been breaks at times; but these breaks have not at any stage brought about anything like a revolution. They are landmarks where new questions have been asked and new modes of answering them have been sought.

Let us then see the backgrounds against which the three systems grew. The background of classical political economy is clear. Classical questions centred on progress and poverty, two conspicuous features of the British economy during the early phase of the industrial revolution. Questions on progress led on to the theory

[4]The term 'epoch' is borrowed from Charles Gide and Charles Rist (*A History of Economic Doctrines* (George G. Harrap, London, 1945), Preface, pp. xiv–xv). The periodization followed by Gide and Rist, however, seems to be based on views on questions rather than on questions as such. Accordingly the authors group the critics of the classical liberal principle, such as Marx, under a separate epoch, while John Stuart Mill is allowed to represent an epoch which is said to mark 'the triumph of the liberal school' as against the early socialists. My epochs, on the other hand, divide themselves in terms of the character of questions asked rather than the views expressed; thus the procedure adopted here puts Ricardo, Malthus, Mill and Marx under one banner, even though their views on questions differ ever so conspicuously. Nor, for that matter does our epoch conform to Schumpeter's definition of 'school', as representing 'one master, one doctrine, personal coherence'. See J. Schumpeter, *History of Economic Analysis* (George Allen & Unwin, London, 1954), p. 470; also 'Keynes, the Economist' in *The New Economics*, ed. Seymour Harris (Dennis Dobson, London, 1947), p. 97. Schumpeter thus speaks of a Ricardo-school, a Marx-school or a Keynes-school, the reference being to the political implications of the respective theories. Our reference here is to the systems of economic theory as such.

of accumulation and innovation. Questions on poverty led on to the theory of population (or as Marx would have it, to the theory of exploitation). Finally, analysis of the interaction between accumulation and population led on to the classical theory of economic growth.

It is not as if the momentum of progress had spent itself in the years preceding the advent of marginalism; in what is regarded as the second phase of the industrial revolution, the British economy experienced a rate of growth which was even higher than in the earlier phase. There was no doubt a depression in the last quarter of the century, the years of the ascendancy of the marginalist system. But the depression was one of prices and profits rather than of production as such.[5] How does one explain the emergence, in this milieu, of a system which totally suppressed the classical questions?

The classical theory of population was weak and had to be abandoned. There was also the emergence of trade unions to reckon with. But these do not explain why there should have been an abandonment of the classical questions altogether. Could it be complacency at the state of the economy? Freedom of trade for which the classical economists fought had been achieved; the last vestiges of protection had been removed by the sixties; the economy was maintaining its momentum of growth in a placid atmosphere of free trade. It could thus be that contemporary economic thinking took growth for granted and turned on relative prices and techniques of production – questions to which the classical answer was weak. This, however, is not a fully satisfactory explanation. It so happens that the new wave of economic theory appeared not only in England but also in two other centres, Vienna and Lausanne, at about the same time. While the explanation may hold for England, it may not hold for the Continent. The explanation of the marginalist challenge – it was indeed a challenge – may have to be sought elsewhere than in the shift of events. It is arguable that the marginalists had misgivings over certain social implications of the classical propositions. And since apparently these propositions rested

[5]See on this Pauline Gregg, *A Social and Economic History of Britain 1760–1972*, 7th edition (Harrap, London, 1973), part II, ch. XVIII. 'Industry remained in a condition of prosperity until 1873. In that year began the great depression which, with a temporary and partial lifting between 1880 and 1882 and between 1886 and 1889, lasted until 1896. Its strangest feature was that, while general agreement existed as to the fact of depression, by most of the criteria generally applied to industry it was a period of prosperity . . . It was a depression, not of production, but of prices and profits.' p. 367.

on the labour theory of value, they chose to concentrate on a field of enquiry where the labour theory was clearly weak and where the new technique which they had discovered was most effective. The field that they chose was thus that of relative prices and resource allocation. In the event the typical classical questions on accumulation and growth were just left aside.[6] This is a possible explanation. We shall have occasion to go into it.

The provocation that led to what we have called the Keynesian epoch is straightforward. Keynes reacted to a state of obstinate depression that gripped the economies of the West in the later years of the inter-war period. The situation was in sharp contrast with what the classical economists had faced. If classical political economy was inspired by the vigour that the British economy showed in the early phase of the industrial revolution, Keynesian economics was provoked by the stagnation into which the economy fell as the forces making for the industrial revolution – accumulation and innovation – were withering away.

Object of the Study

This is not a book on the history of economic theory. Its aim is much more modest; I wish only to suggest a perspective for viewing the development of economic theory. This, I claim, is very important. Much of the controversy which has afflicted the economist's profession over the years could be avoided if it were realized that the different systems of economic theory which the epochs represent were designed to answer different sorts of questions that appeared significant at different points of time. If the marginalist technique fails to explain the growth of an economy as a sequence in time, one must not quarrel over this failure; the technique was not designed for this purpose. It is enough if it succeeds in explaining how the prices and outputs of individual goods are determined in the market, and how these prices and outputs are related to one another. For these are the sorts of questions that the technique was designed to answer.

---

[6]The questions indeed remained neglected for not less than eighty years until they were revived in the post-war period – this time largely under pressure from underdeveloped countries.

The systems of economic theory that I propose to study are incomplete. They deal with *aspects* of an economy. Whether a synthesis of the various systems will ever be attained is doubtful, very doubtful indeed. Remember that economic science differs fundamentally from the physical sciences. The physical universe, taken as a whole, is supposed to exist independently of time. The universe with which economic science deals is a flow over time and with the passage of time new situations arise in the economic field creating new problems. Physicist Stephen Hawking, in a recent lecture, warned his profession about the prospect of an end of theoretical physics 'in the not too distant future'.[7] Whether the end that Hawking visualizes is near or distant is not the point. What is significant is that the boundary of the physicist's universe of discourse is supposed to be limited. This certainly cannot be said of economic science. The economic scientist can count on being able to retain his occupation indefinitely, thanks to the peculiarity of economic reality – its changing character. This also is why one would feel sceptical about the possibility of the construction of a unified system of economic theory. In economics it appears one has to be content with partial theories, even though one knows that being partial they are in their application only approximations. At any rate this is how it is proposed to proceed in this book; my study takes the systems of economic theory as I find them.

My approach in this book is selective. I have taken for my study representative economists in respect of each epoch. The Keynes epoch is of course straightforward; the *General Theory* is the maker of the epoch. I confine myself to the theory of underemployment equilibrium that Keynes offers, fixing on the peculiar feature of the economy of which the theory is a reflection. Thus one of the things that we shall find is that the *General Theory* is not so general after all as its author claims it to be.

So far as the classical epoch is concerned, the main representatives are Adam Smith, David Ricardo and Karl Marx. It is clear that Smith's *Wealth of Nations* is the source from which much of what is known as classical political economy was derived. It is also clear that David Ricardo gave the system a coherent structure and was the central figure during the heyday of classical political economy. Karl Marx is the odd man out. He does not properly belong to the

---

[7]See Stephen Hawking's inaugural lecture at Cambridge University – *Is the End in Sight for Theoretical Physics?* (Cambridge, 1980).

classical period; the last ten years of his life were years of consolidation of the marginalist system. The best plea that one could offer for placing him as a representative of the classical epoch is that his economics was classical by his own definition of classical political economy. Marx asked much the same questions as Smith or Ricardo did, albeit his answers were different.

Who should represent the marginalist epoch? In order to highlight the salient features of the marginalist system as contrasted with those of its predecessor I have defined it rather strictly in this book; I have taken marginalism in its pure form, as a system which is concerned exclusively with the allocation of *given* resources. The economy in this system is assumed to be stationary by hypothesis. The relations studied are thus static relations; time is eliminated.[8] The founders of the system – Jevons, Menger and Walras – are of course taken as the main representatives of the epoch. There are two other economists, among the pioneers, to whom we shall pay attention, especially in the context of the theory of factor prices. They are J. B. Clark and Philip Wicksteed. I believe that these pioneers, between them, cover the main lines of development of marginalist economics, as defined here.

It is usual to designate marginalist economics as 'neo-classical', thereby suggesting that there obtains a link between it and classical political economy. The term surely is misplaced, if the interpretation here offered is correct. Marginalist economics, as I view it, is distinct from classical political economy not only in respect of form but also in respect of purpose and content. It will be indeed my endeavour in this book to show how distinct it is. I have thus avoided the term 'neo-classical' in my description of the marginalist epoch. There is, however, one school of economic theory belonging to the epoch which would perhaps welcome the label, the Cambridge school which Alfred Marshall built. Marshall was undoubtedly one of the originators of the marginal principle and could be counted as one of the leaders of the epoch. However, he felt uncomfortable about the static approach of his contemporaries and constructed a method of his own which explicitly recognized economic activity as a process in time, much as classical political economy did. He was anxious, in spite of his affiliation to marginalism, not to sever his link with the classics. I have accordingly considered Marshall's

---

[8]This, let it be noted, explains why the protagonists of the system observe a similarity between economics and the physical sciences.

system separately, as a deviation from the general marginalist approach, to see how far it goes towards a 'neo-classical' synthesis.

I begin naturally with classical political economy, the first task being to define it. It will be noticed that it has not been an easy task; different writers have defined the term in different ways. I have adopted a definition, following Marx, which takes account of its basic characteristics. Thus it is that special attention has been paid to the classical analysis of class relations as they are supposed to develop in the course of the progress of an economy. Thus also it is that priority has been given, as the arrangement of the chapters will show, to distribution and growth over value.

In the chapter on marginalist economics (excluding Alfred Marshall) the main purpose has been to bring out the salient features of the system and to show how far removed they are from those that characterize classical political economy. I have indeed viewed the system as a challenge to classical political economy and have titled the chapter as such. A chapter on Alfred Marshall has been included in view of his special position as one, among the marginalists, who resisted being 'seduced' by the static method. The jurisdiction of Marshall's system is narrow; it is confined to a single industry. Yet by its recognition of a sequential element in economic analysis, it suggests a link with the classical procedure. What is no less important is that the method which Marshall uses shows the way to the innovation that marks the Keynesian epoch. This is dealt with in the penultimate chapter. The final chapter is a summary view of the findings of the survey.

2

Characteristics of
Classical Political Economy

Who Are the Classical Economists?

It is surprising that historians of economic thought do not have a clear-cut answer to this question. Usually the description runs in terms of a period – the period covered by the publication of Adam Smith's *Wealth of Nations* (1776) at one end, and J. S. Mill's *Principles* (1848) at the other end; economists belonging to the period are described as classical economists. In a recent book – *The Classical Economists* – D. P. O'Brien pursues this period-wise description literally.[1] Although he seems inclined to go a little further back, so as to include David Hume (to whom classical economics 'owed a great deal'), and to extend the period beyond 1848, so as to include J. E. Cairnes (though not Karl Marx!), his main thrust is upon the period 1776–1848. He describes *all* economists belonging to the period as classical economists; the list thus includes such men as Samuel Bailey and W. F. Lloyd, who might as well be regarded as precursors of marginalist economics. To place all economists belonging to a particular period under the same banner, irrespective not only of their persuasion but also of their interests and approach, is surely misleading.

J. Schumpeter gives a pedantic description of the classical period: 'first, fresh activity that struggled hopefully with the deadwood; then things settled down and there emerged a typical classical situation, summed up in the typically classic achievements of J. S. Mill, who underlined the fact by his attitude of speaking from the vantage ground of established truth. Then followed stagnation – a

[1]D. P. O'Brien, *The Classical Economists* (Oxford University Press, Oxford, 1975), ch. 1.

state that was universally felt to be one of maturity of the science, if not one of decay; a state in which those who knew, were substantially in agreement.'[2] But what was the agreement about? Was there any universal agreement at all on any issue among economists of the period? Schumpeter's description leaves these questions unanswered.

Nor is Keynes's definition any more edifying. Keynes lists all those economists as 'classical' who are supposed to accept what is known as Say's law. His definition thus transcends any particular period and includes under the heading 'classical' such economists as Alfred Marshall and A. C. Pigou, while it excludes Robert Malthus and Karl Marx. The definition is based on a certain attribute. But it is too personalized; the attribute which Keynes chooses is designed just to differentiate his own economics from that of those whom he opposes. The criterion that Keynes adopts to define 'classical economics' may serve his own purpose well enough; but it has no use for the historian of economic theory. To him surely the specific historical context in which the system grew – the period – is important.

For an appreciation of the specific character of classical political economy, one has inevitably to turn to Karl Marx, the author of the term. Marx, it will be remembered, coined the term 'classical' to distinguish it from 'vulgar' political economy. 'Once for all I may here state', writes Marx, 'that by classical Political Economy, I understand that economy which, since the time of W. Petty, has investigated the real relations of production in Bourgeois society in contradiction to vulgar economy, which deals with appearances only'.[3] Now, what are 'appearances', and what is the reality that lies behind them? It seems clear that by appearances Marx means exchange relations between *things*, as expressed in the market. Commodity prices are a market phenomenon. So are wages, profits and rent, each related to a factor – wages to labour, profits to capital and rent to land. Vulgar political economy apparently is ascribed to a system which moves round these phenomena. There is evidence that Marx considers all economic theory which relates commodity prices to factor prices as vulgar; he indeed detects a 'vulgar' element in Adam Smith's theory, in so far as the latter explains commodity

[2] J. Schumpeter, *History of Economic Analysis* (George Allen & Unwin, London, 1954), p. 380.
[3] Karl Marx, *Capital* (Foreign Languages Publishing House, Moscow, 1958), vol. I, p. 81n.

prices in terms of cost of production, or in other words, in terms of factor prices.

Yet this is not all. If it were, few systems of economic theory would be classed as 'vulgar'. It is indeed quite a general procedure in economic theory to explain market phenomena in terms other than those that appear within the market. What, one may ask, would Marx have to say about the system of economic theory which takes utility as the source of value? What is the status of what is usually, though misleadingly, called 'neo-classical economics' and what I have preferred to call 'marginalist economics'? In the marginalist theory of value surely there is no circular reasoning; both commodity prices and factor prices are derived from one ultimate source, utility. Yet, it seems clear that Marx, if he were to write after Jevons and Walras, would place their system in the 'vulgar' category. A system which confines itself exclusively to relations between commodities would surely satisfy the test of 'vulgar political economy', as Marx defines it.[4] One can indeed get Marx's attitude to marginalist economics in this respect from his observations on Samuel Bailey. Writing on the 'Disintegration of the Ricardian School', Marx specifically refers to Bailey, one of the early dissenters, and observes: 'Bailey clings to the form in which the exchange value of the commodity as commodity appears, manifests itself. . . . The most superficial form of exchange value, that is the *quantitative* relationship in which commodities exchange with one another, *constitutes* according to Bailey, their value. The advance from the surface to the core of the problem is not permitted'.[5] Does not the same stricture apply to the system of Jevons and Walras?

Recognition of labour as the source of value, with its corollary, class conflict, is on Marx's definition the specific criterion by which one must distinguish classical political economy. I accept this criterion. I identify classical political economy with the system of economic theory which looks, beneath the veil of market phenomena, for the human relations that emerge in the process of

---

[4]See Karl Marx, *Theories of Surplus Value* (Foreign Languages Publishing House, Moscow, 1971), vol. III, pp. 500–3, for a further clarification of the matter. 'Classical Political Economy', Marx observes, 'seeks to reduce the various fixed and mutually alien forms of wealth to their inner unity by means of analysis and to strip away the form in which they exist independently alongside one another. It seeks to grasp the inner connection in contrast to the multiplicity of outward forms . . . the vulgar economists, on the other hand, feel completely at home precisely with the *alienated form* in which the different parts of value confront one another.'

[5]Ibid., pp. 139–47.

production and exchange in a capitalist society. In separating out the classical system from marginalist economics, I shall adopt this criterion; as we shall see, the latter deals exclusively with price ratios and eschews class relations altogether.[6]

However, since I define an epoch with reference to the sorts of questions with which it is associated, I shall pay special attention to the central phenomenon round which the questions revolved. Class relations no doubt form a major aspect of the classical economists' enquiry ever since Adam Smith's *Wealth of Nations*; yet my special emphasis will be on the theory of growth. For growth of wealth is the central phenomenon in the context of which the classical economists viewed the behaviour of social classes. Classical political economy grew in England against the background of the industrial revolution; it is indeed the product of the industrial revolution. Adam Smith wrote on the eve of the industrial revolution; Ricardo and Malthus wrote in the midst of it; while John Stuart Mill's England saw, in the wake of the revolution, forces gathering towards the formation of labour unions. Growth naturally forms the subject matter of classical political economy. Yet its analysis of the dynamics of the capitalist system of production brought to the fore a certain conflict of interest among the broad 'classes' into which the society was seen to be divided – an antithesis between profits and rent on the one hand and between wages and profits on the other. These 'inner relations of production' are what Karl Marx highlights as the criterion for defining classical political economy. If this criterion is accepted, Marx himself comes in very much as an economist of the classical school. He indeed does; my 'classical' epoch begins with Adam Smith, and it includes Karl Marx.[7] The core of Marx's system, like that of Smith and Ricardo, is accumulation and growth. If he did not mention growth as such in his characterization of classical political economy, it obviously is because he took it for granted.

---

[6]Walras, for example, very deliberately confines economic theory proper to the study of relations between things, and eschews from its purview relations between persons, or between persons and things. 'Pure economics', he says, 'is in essence, the theory of the determination of prices under a hypothetical regime of perfectly free competition.' L. Walras, *Elements of Pure Economics*, 4th edition, (George Allen & Unwin, London, 1954), Preface, p. 40. Also see Lessons 2 and 3 for an analysis of the scope of economic science, as Walras views it.

[7]Marx's listing, so far as the British classical school is concerned, goes back to W. Petty who, long before Smith, put forward what is often called the 'man-against-nature' approach

Classical Questions

What, then, are the 'classical' questions? It is clear that the questions relate to the properties of a growing economy. Application of labour to resources with which nature has endowed man is the starting point of classical political economy, and its implication is its task to unravel. What use man makes of these resources; what obstacles he faces in meeting the requirements of a growing population; how he overcomes these obstacles on his way to economic progress; how growth affects class relations in the society and how these relations in their turn react on growth; whether, finally, there is any limit to growth[8] – these are the basic questions which the classical economists asked and sought to answer. Classical economic analysis runs in terms of cost and surplus – this latter being recognized as the growth-propelling element in the economy. Value comes in, as part of the system, chiefly in the context of the measurement of this surplus; it occupies a subsidiary position in the system, not the central position, as it does in marginalist economics.

The type of questions in which the classical economists were chiefly interested is seen from discussions that used to be held at the London Political Economy Club. The Club was founded in 1821 apparently at the instance of Ricardo and had on its roll most of the more important economists of the classical school. The questions centred chiefly on capital, profit and the growth of wealth; it is evident that the members drew largely from Adam Smith's *Wealth*. Answers, however, differed. It is interesting to note that the problem of gluts, which had figured so prominently in the history of economic theory and on which Malthus and Ricardo differed so conspicuously, came up for discussion in the very first year of the Club. 'Has machinery a tendency to diminish the demand for labour?' – yet another question of importance for the history of

---

to political economy. Yet I propose to leave him out. It is true that Petty anticipated in some essential way Smith's concept of wealth and value, and of surplus; but his treatment of these matters was not such as would contribute to the building up of a system in a manner in which Smith's treatment does. It is thus from Smith that Ricardo, the pillar of the classical school, derived inspiration. Moreover, since in any case my object is not to present a history of economic theory, but rather to bring out the salient features of the various schools, references to representative authors are all that we need.

[8] 'Towards what ultimate point is society tending by its industrial progress? When the progress ceases, in what condition are we to expect that it will leave mankind?' J. S. Mill, *Principles of Political Economy*, ed. W. J. Ashley (Longmans, London, 1920), p. 746.

economic theory – was taken up in the following year. On this also views differed. It appears that Ricardo originally held the view that labour-saving machinery was an unmixed good. Subsequently, however, he changed this view and inserted the famous chapter, 'On Machinery', in the third edition of his *Principles*. J. L. Mallet records in his diaries that the change was due to his persuasion.[9] Mallet's verdict on how the members of the Club differed on economic issues is significant. 'I do not apprehend', he says, 'if we were in the habit of voting *aye* and *no* on questions proposed, that there would have been half-a-dozen occasions, since the establishment of the Club six years ago, in which anything like unanimity would have prevailed.'[10]

The classical economists took the capitalist system as a framework for their analysis of distribution and growth. They recognized the full implication of the dissociation of labour from property ownership, which capitalism brought in. The most significant feature of the system is that decision making in the field of production and distribution lay solely in the hands of the owner of capital. While competition as between capitalists as such was granted, the institution, they recognized, prevented mobility as between workers on the one hand and capitalists on the other. The framework of classical political economy is the system of capitalism as it operated in reality; competition was allowed in resource allocation in the field of production, but it was barred when it came to the determination of the share of the product as between classes. On all this there was full agreement among the classical economists, including Karl Marx. Yet there were differences in analytical propositions involving answers to questions.

It is by no means that one was right and the other wrong. Differences arose in most cases from a difference in the relative weights given to elements surrounding a given phenomenon. One conspicuous element that so often intervenes to complicate answers to economic questions is time. The impact of an economic event takes time to work itself out fully. The short-run effect of an event is different from its long-run effect, not only in terms of magnitude but sometimes also in terms of direction. If Ricardo revised his

[9]See *Political Economy Club, Minutes and Proceedings, 1821–1921* (London, 1921), vol. VI, pp. 211–12. 'This he [Ricardo] told me himself', Mallet records, 'in the kindest and most ingenuous manner.'
[10]Ibid. p. 217. In view of this, it seems clear that Schumpeter's description of a Ricardo-school, as noted earlier (chapter 1, p. 5*n*), is an exaggeration.

theory concerning the effect of machinery upon the employment of labour, it was only to concede that employment might decline in the short run, though not in the long run. The classical controversy between Malthus and Ricardo on gluts could also be explained, partly at any rate, by a difference in the sights that they set in their analysis of the problem; Malthus takes a short-run, monetary view, whereas Ricardo has his eyes fixed on long-run trends. A similar interpretation, one ventures to suggest, applies to the difference, at the pure theory level, between Ricardo and Marx. Both analyse the dynamics of a capitalist economy. Accumulation plays a crucial role in both, and both assume a tendency to a falling rate of profits. However, their perspectives differ; and here it is Ricardo who has the narrower perspective. In Ricardo's system, innovations are an exogenous variable; his long-run stationary state is the logical outcome of nature's resistance to accumulation operating within a given technology. Marx, on the other hand, takes innovations as an endogenous variable. His theory thus comprises such phenomena as technological changes, booms and slumps, growth of monopolies etc. – phenomena which are more far-reaching than Ricardo ever contemplated.

It will be our endeavour later to understand the significance of these theories. The point to note at this stage is that Malthus, as well as Ricardo and Marx, chose to answer the same question, but that their answers turned out to be different. 'What limits growth?', for example, is a question that they ask. Each traces the implication of accumulation of capital. Each sees obstacles in the process of growth. However, Ricardo sees the obstacle in nature's niggardliness, Marx in the behaviour of capital itself,[11] while Malthus sees it in insufficiency of effective demand. Ricardo's system leads up to a long-run tendency to a stationary state, Marx's system to crises, while Malthus envisages immediate possibilities of unemployment and poverty. The models are different, but the nature of the questions which they seek to answer is the same.

Chief Features of the Classical System

Let us now take a summary view of the characteristic features of classical political economy. First, the primacy of capital

---

[11]'*The real barrier* of çapitalist production is capital itself.' Karl Marx, *Capital*, (Moscow, 1959), vol. III, p. 245.

accumulation. The classical economists hold that it is accumulation – 'investment' in modern terminology – that sets the economy in motion; everything else, they argue, proceeds from this initial activity of the capitalists. Demand plays a passive role in their system.[12] Secondly, the classical economists deal with 'aggregates', and not with micro-entities. Their analysis relates to the progress of the aggregate wealth of a nation. As such, thirdly, the concept of value comes in as relevant in the system in so far as the heterogeneous goods that compose the aggregate need to be made homogeneous. The classical economists seek a measure; their 'value' is thus conceived as a magnitude, not as just a ratio.[13] Fourthly, classical political economy acknowledges the existence of classes in a society – the property-owners and the labouring class. The purpose of the classical theory of distribution is to explain how the aggregate output is shared by these classes, not just how the so-called factors of production are valued in the market. All this is in sharp contrast with the approach of the marginalist school.

It is often said that one distinctive characteristic of classical political economy is that it is 'policy-oriented'. D. P. O'Brien makes a special mention of this. Writing on the preoccupations of classical economists he says: 'Another characteristic of their writings which distinguishes them quite clearly from the neo-classical economics

[12]It is interesting to note that the Political Economy Club put up a question in 1824, which runs thus: 'Might not the term *Demand* be excluded with advantage from the science of political economy?' We do not know what the answer was, for the proceedings of the Club do not record it. However, we can see the attitude of the members from the question itself. It is remarkable that Robbins should have missed this important aspect of classical political economy. As a true marginalist, he apparently gives primacy to consumption, and he thinks that classical economists would do so also. (See L. Robbins, the *Theory of Economic Policy*, Macmillan, London, 1952, p. 7.) In support of this claim he quotes Adam Smith as saying: 'Consumption is the sole end and purpose of all production.' (Adam Smith, *Wealth of Nations* (Everyman's Library, 1933), vol. II, p. 155). The quotation, however, does not bear the interpretation that Robbins is inclined to give it. For, as the next sentence in the text shows, it is a 'maxim' which Smith prescribes, not a representation of fact.

[13]This requires a little clarification. Value in economics is a rate of exchange – a rate between one commodity and another. In any event, therefore, it involves a magnitude, a comparison between two quantities. If X exchanges for $2Y$, the value of X is said to be $2Y$, and $2Y$ is of course a magnitude. However, if it is conceived merely as a rate, or a ratio, then a certain vagueness arises in the value concept when the rate changes over time; if X rises in terms of Y, it follows that Y falls in terms of X, and there is no knowing in which of the commodities the change has occurred. The classical economists, in so far as they are concerned with growth, are anxious to overcome this vagueness; they seek a measure of value such that the heterogeneous commodities that enter into exchange could be aggregated, and also that changes in these aggregates occurring, if they do, over time could be registered unambiguously.

which triumphed with the marginal revolution, and also to some extent from the neo-Keynesian developments of Keynes's work . . . was their concern with formulating policy implications.'[14] Now, there is no doubt that the earlier classical economists reacted to the emerging industrial revolution and that their theories were meant to show the deficiencies of the then existing restrictions on enterprise and trade. Adam Smith's theory of division of labour, for example, provided argument against mercantilist restrictions in general, and Ricardo's theory of rent against the Corn Laws in particular. Malthus's theory of population, to which Ricardo subscribed, may also be linked to the English Poor Laws.[15]

Yet, to say that policy orientation as such is a distinguishing characteristic of classical political economy is somewhat misleading. Which system of economic theory is without its policy implications? If theories purport to shed light on answers to problems, as we have argued they do, any theory has to be policy oriented. Keynesian economics is overtly so; Keynes himself would be the last person indeed to countenance any idea of theorizing for its own sake. If classical political economy reacted to problems arising out of growth, Keynesian economics reacted to problems arising out of stagnation.

It could not be said either, despite protestations of some of its adherents,[16] that marginalist economics was at all neutral to policy. It was not. It would not surely be wrong if one were to say that the introduction of the marginalist system, with its emphasis on 'utility' in the determination of prices, and 'productivity' in the determination of wages, was an attempt at a rehabilitation of liberalism in economic policy at a time when its basis was being challenged in terms of the Ricardian theory of distribution. But on all this more later.

---

[14]D. P. O'Brien, *The Classical Economists*, p. 54.
[15]See on this Edwin Cannan, *A History of the Theories of Production and Distribution in English Political Economy*, 3rd edition (P. S. King & Son, London, 1917), ch. IX, sect. 2; also J. Schumpeter, *Economic Doctrines and Method* (English translation, George Allen & Unwin, London, 1954), pp. 80–6.
[16]See, for example, L. Robbins, *The Nature and Significance of Economic Science* (Macmillan, London, 1932), ch. VI.

3

Distribution and Growth

The Problem

Classical political economy, I have argued, centres on growth and distribution. The impetus to growth is provided by capital accumulation and innovation. The former provides sustenance to additional labour that is needed to permit wealth to grow; the latter makes it possible for a given amount of labour to produce more – Smith's 'division of labour' is indeed an aspect of innovation.

The relation of growth and distribution is one of interdependence. While the process of growth and the stage of development affect the distribution of wealth in a society, the pattern of distribution in its turn determines the possibilities of growth. The classical economists take the capitalist system as it actually functions – a system in which the capitalist class ('owners of stock') plays a dominant role in the productive process, hiring labour at wages determined in the market and also, if necessary, land at rent, similarly determined. What is left of the output after payment of wages and rent is profit, which it retains for its own consumption and for accumulation. There is enough competition admitted in the classical system to ensure a tendency to a uniform rate of profit; but, as between the property-owners and the labouring class, mobility is absent. The urge to accumulate is derived from the expectation of profit; the behaviour of profits thus determines the behaviour of the economy.[1]

Where does value stand in this set-up? It seems clear that value has a subsidiary role in the classical system. In fact in his first

[1]The classical economists identify accumulation with investment; institutions separating the act of saving from the act of productive investment were yet to arrive.

exercise,[2] Ricardo worked out his theory of distribution entirely without the intervention of value; he used a corn model where both output and input were represented by one commodity, corn. Later on also he wrote: 'After all, the great questions of Rent, Wages and Profits must be explained by the proportions in which the whole produce is divided between landlords, capitalists, and labourers, and which are not necessarily connected with the doctrine of value.'[3] The same consideration applies to Adam Smith's theory of growth; the propositions of Smith come out easily when both wages and surplus are represented in terms of a single commodity.[4] On the other hand, if Karl Marx, in expounding his theory of capitalist development, puts value right at the centre, he does it only to define the categories that are involved in the process in terms of a chosen standard; his labour theory is not an explanatory hypothesis, it is primarily a definition.

Classical economists needed a *measure* of value, an 'invariable standard' in terms of which heterogeneous commodities could be brought into relation with one another and its progress through time exhibited. The corn model is obviously an abstraction. If Ricardo adopts it as a preliminary exercise, he does it clearly for purposes of exposition. The problem still remains for him to discover if the propositions that proceed from his simple model apply to the real economy where commodities are heterogeneous and they enter into wages and profits in unequal proportions. If the propositions survive the re-examination, value clearly appears as an appendage, though a necessary appendage.

We must now get down to detail. In the account that follows, we shall concentrate on Smith, Ricardo and Marx, who, between them cover most of what classical political economy stands for. The analysis will run in terms of distribution and growth; value will be kept in the cupboard for the time being.

Adam Smith's Growth Theory

Adam Smith's approach is explicitly a 'growth' approach. He calls his book *An Inquiry into the Nature and Causes of the Wealth*

[2]D. Ricardo, 'An Essay on the Influence of a Low Price of Corn on the Profits of Stock' (1815), in *The Works and Correspondence of David Ricardo,* ed. P. Sraffa (Cambridge University Press, 1951), vol. IV.
[3]Letter to McCulloch (June, 1820), ibid., vol. VIII, p. 194.
[4]See, e.g., John Hicks, *Capital and Growth* (Oxford University Press, Oxford, 1965), ch. IV,

of Nations. How does he proceed with his enquiry? We shall take three ingredients of growth theory which figure in Smith's system in the order in which they appear in the book.

First, productivity of labour. This depends, Smith argues, upon 'division of labour'.[5] Further, division of labour itself is a function of the size of the market – in other words, of the scale of production.

Second, the concept of 'real price'. Smith uses the term 'real price' as synonymous with 'value', and defines it in terms of labour. Labour commanded by commodities in the market is supposed to be the *measure* of the values of different commodities 'at all times, and at all places'.[6] This, be it noted, is a definition as much as Marx's 'labour embodied' measure is. However, 'labour commanded', unlike 'labour embodied', is a derivative and does not inhere in commodities in the way in which the latter does; it is derived, on the one hand, from the price of commodities as it tends to be established in the market – 'natural price', as Smith would call it – and the rate of wages prevailing in the market, on the other. If, for example, the price per unit of a commodity x is p and the rate of wages is w, then the quantity of labour that the commodity commands in the market is px/w, irrespective of the quantity of labour embodied in it. So for the aggregate of commodities, provided the exchange relations between them are known otherwise.[7]

Third, accumulation of capital. Smith identifies accumulation of capital with the employment of 'productive labour'[8] – labour which produces *goods* that stay, as distinguished from *services* which 'perish in the very instant of their performance'. The sources of accumulation are rent and profits.[9]

It is possible to build a model of growth on these three ingredients. We shall follow Smith closely in building the model. We shall take the aggregate of commodities, not corn alone, as the base for our

---

pp. 36–40. However, contrary to Hicks's belief, there is no evidence that Smith had himself a corn model in his mind.

[5]'The greatest improvement in the productive powers of labour . . . seem to have been the effects of the division of labour.' Adam Smith, *Wealth of Nations* (Everyman's Library, 1933), p. 4.

[6]Ibid., p. 28.

[7]This is precisely where the 'theory' of value, as an explanatory hypothesis, comes in.

[8]The title of the relevant chapter in the *Wealth of Nations* significantly is: 'Of the Accumulation of Capital, Or of Productive and Unproductive Labour', Book II, ch. III.

[9]The landlords, Smith holds, are no doubt more prone to unproductive expenditure; yet they too accumulate. 'The expense of a great lord feeds more idle than industrious people', ibid., vol. I, p. 297.

growth model; it is clear that Smith would have us do so. We shall, however, assume, for the time being (until we come to Smith's theory of value), that exchange relations between commodities are given and constant. A few specific assumptions will now be made – none out of accord with Smith's general approach.

First, we shall assume that the production period is given (say, a year) and that the capital which is used in the process of production exhausts itself during the period. We are thus led on to a sequence analysis, one production period being linked to another in terms of changes in the stock of capital.

Secondly, capital will be supposed to consist of wage advances only. This is a peculiar Smithian assumption, later taken over by Ricardo and much criticized by Marx. While, Smith argues, from the point of view of an individual industry the cost of 'replacing the stock' or 'compensating the wear and tear of his labouring cattle and other instruments of husbandry' is a part of capital, judged from the point of view of the community, instruments themselves are products, so that 'the whole price still resolves itself either immediately or ultimately into the same three parts of rent, labour and profit.'[10]

Thirdly, we shall assume that wage advances are locked up for the entire production period, as though the entire advance is made at the beginning of the period and recovered at the end of the period.[11]

Finally, we assume that the rate of wages remains constant through time. It is a simplifying assumption; one can modify it if one chooses. However, the assumption is in conformity with Adam Smith's own theory of wages. Smith no doubt recognizes the possibility of accumulation exceeding the rate at which population grows and consequently of a tendency of wages to rise. But it also follows from his analysis that the tendency cannot persist. For, as wages rise beyond the 'natural rate', the rate of accumulation declines and there is also a tendency to an increase in the rate of population growth.[12] The forces are supposed to operate in such

---

[10]Adam Smith, *Wealth of Nations*, vol. I, pp. 44–5.

[11]This is a convenient, not a necessary assumption. The convenience lies in the fact that, on this assumption, capital can be identified with aggregate wages.

[12]'If this demand for labour is continually increasing, the reward of labour must necessarily encourage in such a manner the marriage and multiplication of labourers as may enable them to supply that continually increasing demand by continually increasing population.' Adam Smith, *Wealth of Nations* vol. I, p. 71.

a way that wages ultimately come down to the natural level. Our model will concentrate on this natural rate of wages, ignoring the fluctuations that might take place in any production period, taken in isolation.

We may now write down the equations. Operations start, let us say, with L quantity of labour. Let this labour, together with other resources, produce an aggregate output Q. While in the 'early and rude state of society' the entire output goes to labour, in an 'advanced society' it is split up into wages, rent and profit. These latter are 'deductions' from the output, due to the fact that the ownership of land and of stock has now gone over to two distinct classes – the landlords and the capitalists.[13] Thus,

$$Q = W + R + P$$

where W stands for wages, R for rent and P stands for profit.

Since, as we have noted, separation of rent from profits does not have any significance from the point of the growth theory of Adam Smith, both being sources of accumulation, we can combine the two into what may be called surplus.[14]

Let S stand for surplus. Thus,

$$Q = W + S$$

Suppose now that w is the rate of wages, so that $W = wL$, or $W/w = L$. This means that W commands L quantity of labour, precisely the quantity with which operations started. The system therefore has still S left for the purchase of additional labour. What proportion of it will be used for employment of 'productive' labour depends upon the choice of the owners of land and of stock. If, suppose, a proportion c of S is consumed by these owners, or used unproductively, then $(1 - c)S$ is available for employment of productive labour – in other words, for capital formation. The quantity of additional labour which $(1 - c)S$ commands in the market, $(1 - c)S/w$, let us say, is ΔL. We have then $(L + \Delta L)$ quantity of labour with which to start operations in the next production period. Let $L + \Delta L = L_1$. The next production period, then, starts

[13]Smith does not use the word 'capitalist'; he calls this class 'owners of stock', or often, 'masters'.

[14]It will, however, be seen later that the division of surplus into rent and profits is highly significant from the point of view of Smith's theory of distribution.

with L_1 quantity of labour and ends up with a surplus, which we may call S_1, a proportion, $(1 - c_1)$ of which, let us say, is devoted to the employment of productive labour. The quantity of additional labour that $(1 - c_1)S_1$ commends in the market, $(1 - c_1)S_1/w$, may, as in the previous case, be represented by ΔL_1, and so on for subsequent production periods. The rate of capital formation is thus $\Delta L/L$ in the first period, $\Delta L_1/L_1$ in the second period, and, say, $\Delta L_2/L_2$ in the third, and so on.

Now, put q, q_1, q_2, etc. for the productivity of labour for different production periods. This is where 'division of labour' comes in, for the productivity of labour at any stage in the development of an economy is largely a function of division of labour. We then have $qL(= Y)$ to start with, where Y stands for income. The increment of income during the first production period, let us say, is $\Delta Y(= q\Delta L)$. The rate of growth of income g is then $\Delta Y/Y$ for the first production period. In the same way we would have $g_1 = \Delta Y_1/Y_1$, $g_2 = \Delta Y_2/Y_2$, and so on for subsequent periods, Y_1, Y_2, depending, let us remind ourselves, not only upon L_1, $L_2 \ldots$, but also upon q_1, $q_2 \ldots$, the latter rising with increasing division of labour.[15]

From this it is an easy step to a growth function; given the rate of wages and assuming that the level of wages is such that the labourers consume all that they earn, growth of income is a function of the productivity of labour and the propensity to consume on the part of landlords and capitalists. In a special case, where q and $(1 - c)$ remain constant through time, the economy experiences a steady rate of growth.[16]

Can such a thing happen? Can growth be sustained indefinitely? Is there no limit to growth? Adam Smith's answer to the question is not clear. It is not true that Smith did not recognize the possibility of diminishing returns from land. He certainly did. Referring to investments in a new colony, he says that although initially they

---

[15]In an earlier version ('Adam Smith on Value', *The Indian Economic Review*, August 1960) I had shown Smith's growth theory along this line in terms of employment only. Here an additional variable, labour productivity, is introduced to translate employment growth into income growth. A similar procedure seems to have been adopted by John Hicks. See John Hicks, *Capital and Growth*, pp. 36–8. See also Hla Myint, *Theories of Welfare Economics* (Longmans, London, 1948), ch. II, sect. II.

[16]On the Smithian assumption adopted here, labour–capital ratio is given and constant, so labour productivity comes to be the same thing as capital productivity. Also since $(1 - c)$ is just the rate of savings, growth can be seen alternatively as a function of output–capital ratio and the rate of savings.

may yield high profit, it tends to fall with increasing accumulation. 'When the most fertile and best situated lands have been all occupied, less profit can be made by the cultivation of what is inferior both in soil and situation, and less interest can be afforded for the stock which is so employed.'[17] Yet it is also not true that Smith would consider any possible diminishing returns in agriculture to be an impediment to a steady rate of growth. The scope of division of labour, Smith argues, is general, even though it is less in agriculture than in manufactures. 'The most opulent nations, indeed, generally excel all their neighbours in agriculture as well as in manufactures.'[18] The effect of division of labour is thus allowed to compensate for whatever diminishing returns might arise in agriculture due to nature's constraints.

Adam Smith gives rather more importance to a possible decline in investment opportunities as accumulation proceeds. 'As capitals increase in any country, the profits which can be made by employing them necessarily diminish. It becomes gradually more and more difficult to find within the country a profitable method of employing any new capital.'[19] But of course extension of the market via free trade would remedy the deficiency by calling forth more division of labour. It thus appears that Adam Smith would not rule out a steady rate of growth as a trend over time. Smith mentions the possibility of a progressive state, a stationary state and also a declining state. These are for him hypothetical states which occur under different sets of conditions; the formulation does not seem to have any predictive implication. 'If X, then Y' is the kind of analysis which Smith seems to adopt. It was Ricardo, and later Marx, who adapted their systems of analysis for long-run prediction. To them we now turn.

Ricardo's Theory of Falling Rate of Profits

It is customary to regard David Ricardo as the author of a theory of distribution. Ricardo's chief concern apparently is with the

---

[17] Adam Smith, *Wealth of Nations*, vol. I, p. 82. Schumpeter seems to have overlooked this passage, for he says categorically that 'nowhere did he [Smith] state a law of decreasing returns.' See J. Schumpeter, *History of Economic Analysis*, p. 259.
[18] Adam Smith, *Wealth of Nations*, p. 6.
[19] Ibid., vol. I, p. 316. The proposition appears on the face of it to anticipate Malthus's theory of gluts. In fact, however, it does not. As the context suggests, profits are supposed to fall because wages tend to rise on account of an increasing demand for labour coming

question as to how 'the produce of the earth' is divided among the proprietors of land, owners of capital and the labourers. He says this in a much-quoted sentence in the Preface to his *Principles*: 'To determine the laws which regulate this distribution is the principal problem in Political Economy'.[20] What is, however, very often overlooked in the literature is that Ricardo considers the problem against the background of accumulation and growth; he makes this clear in the very next sentence in the Preface, where he underlines the need for a theory of 'the natural *course* of rent, profit, and wages'.[21] Further, it is no accident that the essay where Ricardo first enunciates his theory of distribution is titled 'An Essay on the Influence of Low Price of Corn on the Profits of Stock'; it is clear that he is interested primarily in the behaviour of profits, for it is the expectation of profit that motivates accumulation of capital and stimulates growth. 'While profits of stock are high, men will have a motive to accumulate.'[22]

In his 'Essay on Profits' (as one may call it, following Sraffa's abbreviation), Ricardo explicitly uses a corn model. Output is in corn. The capitalist farmer, who initiates the productive process, hires labour by making wage advances in corn and hires land by offering rent, also in corn. Output belongs to the farmer by virtue of his ownership of capital; but he has to surrender a part of it towards the payment of wages to labourers and a part towards the payment of rent to the owners of land. The 'Essay' was published in 1815, two years after the enactment of the Corn Laws in England, and was designed with a view to showing how restrictions on the import of corn affected the price of corn and the profits of the capitalists. Ricardo's contention is that these restrictions raise the price of corn and hence the wages of labour in 'price' terms, though not in terms of corn itself, and lower the profits of capitalists, the only beneficiary being the landowning class who now earn a higher rent. The withdrawal of these restrictions would reverse the process, lowering rent and raising profits.

---

from competing capitalists. On the contrary, Adam Smith can be held to have anticipated Say's law. For, elsewhere he says: 'What is annually saved is as regularly consumed as what is annually spent, and nearly in the same time too; but it is consumed by a different set of people.' Ibid., p. 302.

[20] D. Ricardo, *Principles of Political Economy* (Everyman's Library, 1933), Preface.

[21] Emphasis mine. It is important to emphasize this, because there is a feeling in certain quarters that Ricardo did not pay enough attention to growth as such. See, e.g., D. P. O'Brien, *The Classical Economists* (Oxford University Press, Oxford, 1975), p. 214.

[22] D. Ricardo, *Principles* (Everyman's Library, London, 1933), p. 193.

Ricardo's theory of rent, which is the pivot of his theory of distribution is worked out in terms of diminishing returns. Land, 'the original and indestructible powers of the soil', is fixed. Increasing employment of capital and labour has thus a tendency to lower output per unit of capital and labour; there is pressure on land, and rent tends to rise and profits tend to fall.

So far, so good. Where diminishing returns operate in production and there is pressure on land on account of growing population and a growing demand for corn, withdrawal of restrictions on the import of corn surely eases the situation; the margin of cultivation is shifted upward and profits are prevented from falling to the extent that they would if the economy had to depend upon internal production only. And if maintenance of profit, so as to stimulate accumulation, is the objective of policy, there is a strong case for free trade in corn.

However, how far can the economy sustain accumulation even under free trade conditions, so long as population is increasing and technology remains constant? The answer to this leads to Ricardo's theory of growth. In setting out Ricardo's growth theory we follow his corn model here and eschew 'value'. As in the case of Smith's model, production period is assumed to be self-contained, the watershed between two periods being marked by additions to capital and labour; wage advances during a production period, say a year, is assumed to be the only form of capital, the wage rate in corn terms is assumed to be constant at some kind of a subsistence level, and aggregate wages are taken as identical with capital. All this means, again as in Smith's model, that capital is tied to labour in a given ratio, a 'unit' of labour and capital being defined in terms of this given ratio. However, unlike in Smith's model, production is assumed to be subject to diminishing returns, and, further, technology is assumed to be independent of accumulation, and hence given.

Within the framework of these assumptions, Ricardo's verdict on the possibilities of growth is clear and unambiguous. The capitalist is supposed to accumulate, urged by the prospect of profit, expected profit being assumed to be equal to current profit. The additional wage fund (accumulation, that is) available at the beginning of a production period depends upon total profits in the previous period and the propensity of capitalists to 'save' out of profits.[23]

[23]Ricardo apparently regards the landowners as belonging to the consuming class, as Malthus does. Perhaps in their time, this was the rule. However, as we shall see, the possibility of rent being also a source of accumulation does not affect Ricardo's main conclusion.

This fund in its turn determines the additional labour that can be employed during the period at the given wage rate. There no doubt is a tendency to a rise in the wage rate with the progress of accumulation, but, as this happens, population catches up and the supply of labour is adjusted to demand.[24] As accumulation proceeds and employment of more labour accompanies it, aggregate output grows, though at a diminishing rate. What happens to the three shares? Clearly the share of wages increases, for while aggregate wages increase just in proportion to the increase in employment, aggregate output increases less than proportionately. It follows that the share of rent and profits, taken together, declines; how the share of each behaves is not immediately clear. Ricardo argues that the share of rent rises with increasing employment. There is indeed a probability that it should rise as the share of profits would tend to fall.[25] What is crucial, however, is that the rate of profit tends to decline as the economy progresses; even aggregate profits do so at later stages in the process of accumulation.

This last is the basis of Ricardo's famous theory of limit to growth. As profits decline, the urge to accumulate declines also. There thus arrives a stage at which the profits are so low that there is no further urge towards accumulation. Capital ceases to grow, and with it population; the economy reaches a stationary state, where the entire surplus above the wages of labour and the minimum profits set by the consumption standard of the capitalists is reaped by the landowning class. Improvements in the method of production may stem the process; but the tendency persists. These propositions come out sharply on a diagram, where Ricardian rent is shown as the excess of average output over marginal output in relation to a given volume of employment.[26]

[24]As in Smith's model, here also we assume that the adjustment is quick enough to leave the wage rate undisturbed during a given production period. Evidently this is an arbitrary assumption; it would be more realistic if Ricardo had brought in unemployment into his model, as did Karl Marx later.

[25]See on this, J. R. Hicks, 'Ricardo's Theory of Distribution', in Essays in Honour of Lionel Robbins ed. Maurice Peston and Bernard Corry (Weidenfeld and Nicolson, London, 1972), pp. 160-7.

[26]The diagram is based on Kaldor's construction (N. Kaldor, Essays on Value and Distribution (Gerald Duckworth, London, 1960), pp. 211-15). While, however, Kaldor proceeds immediately from average and marginal curves and shows the distribution of output in 'per unit' terms, I have chosen to derive the average and marginal outputs from a 'total output' curve. One thus gets a 'total profit' curve, which is an advantage. I have also extended the analysis further, to indicate the passage to Ricardo's theory of growth.

In figure 1, let total output be measured along the Y-axis and the quantity of labour (or capital) be measured along the X-axis. Let OQ be the 'total output' curve, which slopes upward and is concave, showing that, while with every increase in the employment of labour (or capital) the total output increases, it increases at a diminishing rate. Let also OW be the 'total wage' curve – a straight line, making an angle with the X-axis – which represents the given wage rate.

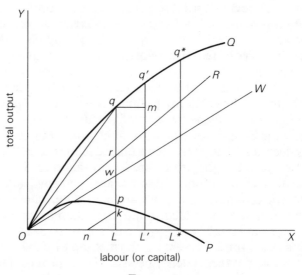

FIGURE 1

Take a point q on OQ; join Oq. Draw OR parallel to the tangent on OQ at q. Also draw qL perpendicular to OX, cutting OR at r and OW at w. The marginal output is then given by the angle that the tangent at q makes with OX, or in other words by $\tan\angle ROX$, while the average output is given by $\tan\angle qOX$. qr/OL, then, is the rent per unit of labour, so that qr is the total rent, and since wL is the total wage, rw is the total profit. Further, take a point q^* on OQ, such that the tangent at q^* is parallel to OW. Draw q^*L^* perpendicular upon OX. OL^*, then, represents a volume of employment at which the marginal output is just equal to the wage rate, at which therefore there is no profit. Now, take a point p on qL, such that $pL = rw$. OP, the locus of p, is then the total profit curve, of which we are in search, as providing a clue to the Ricardian theory of growth. It starts from O, rises upward to a point and then delcines, until it cuts OX at L^*, where profit is zero.

If capitalists alone accumulate, as Ricardo presumably assumes, the mechanism of growth can be exhibited on our diagram thus: Take a point k on pL, such that kL is the amount that the capitalists accumulate out of their profits. Draw kn parallel to OW, and let it meet OX at n. If OL is the volume of employment for our base period, then nL will be the additional employment that the economy will have for the next period. Take a length $LL' = nL$ along OX. Draw $L'q'$ perpendicular upon OX to meet OQ at q'. Draw also qm perpendicular upon $q'L'$ to meet it at m, so that $qm = LL'$. We have then LL'/OL as the rate of growth of employment for our given production period, and $q'm/qL$ as the rate of growth of output.

It is now easy to see that beyond the level of employment for which total profits are at a maximum, the rate of growth in the Ricardian economy should invariably be declining, for each production period, for two reasons. First, the wage fund will be declining unless of course the consumption propensity of the capitalists is perverse.[27] Secondly, labour productivity will be declining; there is diminishing return to increasing employment. The process will continue until a level of employment is reached for which the total profits will be just equal to the minimum consumption of the capitalist.

As in Smith's model, here also growth depends upon the rate of accumulation, supported by the growth of population. However, whereas Smith recognizes innovations as a concomitant of accumulation, and thus allows growth to continue despite nature's resistance, Ricardo brings diminishing return into the forefront of his model and relegates innovations to a subsidiary position. Smith thus sees the possibility of a steady growth, while Ricardo's model exhibits a steadily declining rate of growth, with a stationary state as the ultimate destination.

What happens if the landowning class also accumulate? Hitherto, following Ricardo, we have assumed that it is out of profits alone that the wage fund is derived. Of course, this cannot be taken as a general rule; landowners' rent also is a surplus, and there is no reason why a fraction of it could not be withdrawn from consumption

---

[27]Indeed even if it is perverse for a time, the general tendency to a decline in the wage fund remains.

and be allowed to go in for capital formation. We have seen that Adam Smith grants this possibility. If Ricardo does not take the possibility explicitly into account, it may be because he thought it would be contrary to experience. Yet surely this is not all; he knew also that inclusion of the landowning class as possible contributors to the wage fund would not make any difference to the growth pattern which he envisaged. The fact is that the existence of surplus is a necessary condition for accumulation, it is not a sufficient condition. While the ability to accumulate is related to the volume of surplus, the urge to accumulate depends entirely upon profits. As profits tend towards zero, accumulation peters out, irrespective of what the volume of surplus is. Imagine that the ownership of land is transferred from the landowning class to the capitalist class. What happens then? The technical condition of production remains the same. The wage rate is given and remains constant as before. The volume of employment which yields maximum surplus remains the same. Nothing indeed is altered, except, as Ricardo would put it, that the capitalists now 'live like gentlemen'. On our diagram, the point L^* sets the limit to growth in any case. For here the additional output as shown by the tangent at q^* is just equal to the wage rate. Any further employment involves loss.

Marx's Alternative Formulation

Marx, too, has a theory of falling rate of profits. He too, like Ricardo, analyses the dynamics of a capitalist economy, wherein accumulation and falling profits play a crucial role. Both make predictions concerning the ultimate destination of a capitalist economy. Yet there are differences, important differences, in the two approaches. The differences stem essentially from the fact that Marx takes as his frame of reference a full-fledged industrial economy, while Ricardo, as we know, takes agriculture. New elements thus enter into Marx's scheme of analysis.

First, accumulation in Marx's system represents not merely wage goods, but also machines and raw materials. The economy is seen as consisting of two sectors, one producing capital goods, including raw materials, and the other producing consumption goods, including wage goods. The process of accumulation is identified as a progressive increase in the net output of capital goods relative to wage goods.

Hence, secondly, Marx brings machines and raw materials, advanced by the capitalists and used up in the process of production, explicitly into account while defining output; Marx's 'output' thus includes depreciation.

Thirdly, in the analytical model developed by Marx, rent merges into profits.[28] There are thus two categories of income in the economy – wages and surplus. Wages are paid to the labouring class, and surplus is appropriated by the capitalists as profit.

Fourthly, the wage rate, in Marx's system, is held constant at subsistence level, not through births and deaths, but in terms of variations in the volume of unemployment. Marx assumes that there exists a pool of unemployed ('reserve army of labour', as he calls it) in the agriculture sector, on which the capitalists can draw in case, as accumulation proceeds, there is any tendency to a rise in wages. Only when the pool tends to be exhausted can the wage rate rise beyond subsistence. However, the capitalists prevent this tendency either by reducing the rate of accumulation, or, where possible, by introducing labour-saving devices in the productive process.

So, finally, we come to one of the most significant elements in Marx's system, innovation. Marx gives innovation a crucial position in his analytical structure, as does Schumpeter later. Innovations in Marx's model of growth are an endogenous variable; they are supposed to be labour saving, and are induced by forces making for a tendency of wages to rise.

Does Marx admit diminishing returns? This is an important question, for it is bound up with his theory of falling rate of profits. Paul Samuelson describes Marx as 'Ricardo without diminishing returns',[29] and he has no difficulty in proving that Marx's theory of falling rate of profits is false within his own assumptions. It is

[28]Land, presumably, is assumed to be owned by the capitalists themselves; it is a minor element in industrial production anyway. In the context of agriculture, however, Marx introduced 'ground rent' as an item which the 'capitalist' farmer has to pay to the landowners. He urges, however, that, with growing accumulation, ground rent *per unit of capital* has a tendency to fall, 'although its absolute mass increases and may also increase proportionately more than industrial profit' (Karl Marx, *Capital* (Foreign Language Publishing House, Moscow, 1959), vol. III, pp. 237–8). It is interesting to note that Ricardo's verdict on this is different. In his 'Essay on Profits', Ricardo presents a table which exhibits rent as 'increasing in its ratio to the capital applied on land' with increasing accumulation (D. Ricardo, *Works*, vol. IV, p. 17). The fact, however, is that the effect of accumulation on rent per unit of capital is indeterminate, depending on the shape of the product curve.

[29]*The Collected Scientific Papers of Paul Samuelson*, ed. Joseph Stiglitz (Massachusetts Institute of Technology, Massachusetts, 1966), p. 341.

true that there is no place for Ricardian diminishing returns in Marx's system – land is no limiting factor here. It is also true, as we shall see, that the procedure that Marx adopts in devising his theory of profits does not suggest any overt recognition of diminishing returns of any sort. Yet, to leave the matter at that would be wrong. There is, one would suggest, implicit in the nature of accumulation, as viewed by Marx, the idea of diminishing returns – diminishing returns due to a disproportionate use of factors. Marx does not spell it out, but it must be there. Since, as the economy grows, there is increasing employment of capital per man, there is no reason why the rate at which the total output increases should not be diminishing. At any rate this is how we would like to interpret Marx.

The decks having been cleared, we may now write down Marx's equations. We use his own symbols, where c stands for machines and raw materials used up in the process of production,[30] 'constant capital', in Marx's terminology; v for wages of labour, or 'variable capital'; s for surplus. Correspondingly, c_1, v_1, s_1 stand for constant capital, variable capital and surplus in respect of the capital goods industry; and c_2, v_2, s_2 stand for constant capital, variable capital and surplus in respect of the consumption goods industry.

All these entities are measured in terms of labour embodied, irrespective of the manner in which the diverse goods that constitute them are exchanged in the market. Value of goods is identified by Marx with labour embodied, and has to be distinguished from 'price', as it is determined in the market. Labour embodied in commodities is thus *assumed* here as a measuring rod.

Accumulation, or 'extended reproduction', as Marx would call it, means that $v_1 + s_1 > c_2$, or in other words, output in the capital goods industry exceeds depreciation in the two sectors, taken together. When $v_1 + s_1 = c_2$, we have a stationary state – a state of 'simple reproduction', as Marx calls it.[31] As the economy grows, *via* accumulation, the proportion of constant capital employed in production grows also relatively to variable capital. It is the relation between c, v and s, as it emerges in the process of growth, that concerns Marx.

---

[30]We continue with the assumption of self-contained production periods, so that we may not be bothered by carry-over of stocks.

[31]When output in the capital-goods industry just equals depreciation, $c_1 + v_1 + s_1 = c_1 + c_2$, or $v_1 + s_1 = c_2$. The condition of equilibrium for simple reproduction is that the total surplus value *minus* capitalists' consumption just equals depreciation, whereas for extended reproduction it is that the former exceeds the latter; labourers do not save anyway.

Total (gross) output $= c + v + s$. Of this, v is paid out to labour, c just maintains itself through replacement, and s is appropriated by the capitalists as profit. Now, in so far as c includes machines, a part of it is used up in a process of production, while a part stays.[32] Assuming, however, that the entire stock of 'constant capital' is used up in the process of production, the rate of profit is equal to $s/(c + v)$, or $s/v(1 - c/(c + v))$.[33] As the economy grows, $c/(c + v)$ rises, by hypothesis. In so far, therefore, as s/v remains constant, there is a tendency of profits to fall. This is Marx's famous theory of falling rate of profits.

Now, why should s/v remain constant while the ratio of capital to labour employed in production is rising? When capital per man increases, output per man increases also. Hence s must rise, unless the rate of wages is allowed to rise along with a rise in the productivity of labour. Here is the difficulty which Marx's theory of falling rate of profits is supposed to face. If, as Marx would contend, the rate of wages remains more or less constant normally, s/v should have a tendency to rise as accumulation proceeds. Thus, while in the process of growth $c/(c + v)$ tends to rise, there is a tendency in s/v also to rise. What the joint effect will be upon the rate of profits depends upon the relative strength of the two forces. Can it happen that the force making for a fall in the rate of profits should at all outweigh the force making for a rise? Can the movement in $c/(c + v)$ outstrip the movement in s/v? This is where the condition of production becomes relevant.[34]

We have argued that there is diminishing return implicit in the concept of accumulation that Marx proposes; it follows from a

[32] c is specially significant in Marx's system; it represents the instrument through which the capitalists are supposed to 'exploit' labour. Marx takes Smith severely to task for omitting this item. 'Adam Smith', he complains, 'tries to spirit the constant part of the capital value away from the commodity value' (Karl Marx, *Capital*, vol. II, p. 372.)

[33] $s/(c + v) = (s/v)(v/(c + v)) = (s/v)(1 - c/(c + v))$.

[34] Joan Robinson's scepticism regarding Marx's theory of falling rate of profits arises from just this consideration. She argues that it is most unlikely that the rise in s relative to v, with wage rate constant, should be overborne by the rise in the value of $c/(c + v)$, particularly when innovations are granted as an associate of accumulation. Mrs Robinson, however, admits diminishing returns in Marx's scheme, as the arithmetical example, that she provides, suggests (see Joan Robinson, *An Essay on Marxian Economics* (Macmillan, London, 1942), pp. 43–5). Marx, on the other hand, is emphatic on the issue. 'This capitalist mode of production produces a progressive relative decrease of the variable capital as compared to the constant capital, and consequently a continuously rising organic composition of the total capital. The immediate result of this is that the rate of surplus value, at the same, or even a rising, degree of labour exploitation, is represented by a continually falling general rate of profit. (Karl Marx, *Capital*, vol. III, p. 208–9).

disproportionate employment of capital upon labour. In principle this is not different from Ricardo's diminishing return which follows from a disproportionate employment of capital and labour upon land. And if Marx had allowed wages to rise in the manner in which Ricardo allowed rent to rise, falling rate of profits would be an easy deduction. Can the rate of profits be still falling, when the wage rate is held constant? Is Marx's theory of profits consistent with his theory of wages? This is the problem.

Let us simplify the problem by assuming that the employment of labour remains fixed, while the employment of capital per man is increasing. In figure 2, capital is measured along the X-axis, while total (net) output is measured along the Y-axis. The total output curve OQ is upward sloping and concave (much as Ricardo's total output curve is), showing diminishing return with increasing employment of capital upon a fixed quantity of labour. OW measures the total wage, which remains constant whatever the amount of capital employed. Thus the total wage line WW' is parallel to the X-axis. Draw a tangent from W on OQ, touching it at T. Draw TK perpendicular on OX, cutting WW' at R.

Thus, when OK amount of capital is employed, TK is the total net output $(v+s)$, TR is the total profit, and TR/WR, or $\tan\angle TWR$, is the rate of profit. It can now be easily shown that beyond K, increasing employment of capital leads to a progressive fall in the rate of profit. Take, for example, a point T' to the right of T, on

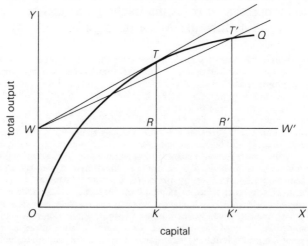

FIGURE 2

OQ. Join WT' and draw $T'K'$ parallel to TK, meeting OX at K' and WW' at R'. We find, then, that OK' is the amount of capital employed, and $\angle T'WR'$, which is less than $\angle TWR$, is the corresponding rate of profit. A larger accumulation is thus associated with a lower rate of profit. The conclusion remains even if we relax the hypothesis and admit variations in the employment of labour; so long as capital per man is increasing, there must be a tendency in the long run to a fall in the rate of profits. If the rate of wages tends to rise, as it may at times, due to the depletion of the pool of unemployed, the tendency is accentuated.

What is the bearing of all this on Marx's theory of growth? Would his economy obey the Ricardian rule? Would it, considering that here labour itself is supposed to have a positive growth rate, slip into a steady state, with a growth rate equalling the growth of population, even as the Ricardian economy, where land has a zero growth rate, slips into a stationary state? No, says Marx, and he brings in other variables to show that growth in a capitalist economy does not have a smooth course at all. The capitalist accumulates. In the process of accumulation, while the economy grows, the rate of profits tends to fall, yet aggregate profits continue to rise. However, the demand for labour eventually presses on the pool of unemployed. The pressure may indeed be such as to overbear accretions to the pool through population growth, thus creating scarcity in the labour market. The rate of wages, then, tends to rise.[35] The result is that even aggregate profits tend to decline.[36] At this stage the capitalists scale down the rate of accumulation, thus causing a deceleration in the rate of growth. There is thus depression in economic activity, and hence unemployment. Further, as wages rise and profits tend to fall, the capitalists are urged on to innovate; and once one firm succeeds, the innovation spreads gradually to the entire area; the cost-reducing device becomes general.[37] This

[35]Marx clearly admits the possibility (see Karl Marx, *Capital*, vol. I, ch. XXV). Here again he differs from early classical economists who, depending upon their theory of population, rule out any long-run tendency to a rise in the wage rate.

[36]This is easily seen in figure 2.

[37]'No capitalist ever voluntarily introduces a new method of production, no matter how much more productive it may be, and how much it may increase the rate of surplus value, so long as it reduces the rate of profit. Yet every such new method of production cheapens the commodities. Hence the capitalist sells them originally above their prices of production, or, perhaps, above their value. He pockets the difference between their costs of production and the market prices of the same commodities produced at higher costs of production.

stimulates economic activity and accelerates the rate of accumulation. The growth path that Marx envisages is thus marked by booms and depressions, the amplitude of which has a tendency to increase as the economy becomes more and more mechanized. Rather than slipping into a steady state, Marx's economy moves jerkily towards what he describes as 'Crisis'.[38]

He can do this because . . . his method of production stands above the social average. But competition makes it general and subject to the general law. There follows a fall in the rate of profit – perhaps just in this sphere of production, and eventually it achieves a balance with the rest – which is, therefore, wholly independent of the will of the capitalist.' (Karl Marx, *Capital*, vol. III, p. 259). This is just the type of analysis that Schumpeter adopts in his theory of economic development, and he acknowledges his affinity to Marx in this respect (see J. Schumpeter, *The Theory of Economic Development* (English translation, Harvard University Press, Cambridge, Massachusetts, 1932), p. 60n).

[38]Marx is probably the first economist to have developed a theory of business cycle. Crises mark the critical depression phase of the cycle, and are characterized by over-production, surplus capital, depreciation of capital values, speculation, unemployment, and so on (see Karl Marx, *Capital*, vol. III, part III, ch. XV).

4

Classical Theories of Value

Meaning of Value

We must now release value from the cupboard in which it has been lying so far. We know that the classical economists deal with aggregates. The goods that form the aggregate are heterogeneous. As such they are not additive; they have to be brought into relation with one another in terms of a common standard before they can be aggregated. The classical economists from Smith to Marx have an aggregation problem, and hence a problem of the valuation of goods. In my account of the classical theories of growth I have so far avoided the problem. In dealing with Smith's theory of growth I took relative prices as given, arguing as if there exists some mysterious way in which goods come to bear a constant relation with one another. Ricardo's theory was presented in physical terms on a one-commodity model, while in the case of Marx I allowed myself to adopt an arbitrary standard of measurement – labour embodied in goods – irrespective of how the goods which comprise the aggregate are valued in the market. All this is to emphasize how in classical political economy the problem of valuation figures as a subsidiary one, subsidiary to the main problem of distribution and growth. It is not that the classical economists themselves ignored the problem; they were in fact very much involved in it, although on this score, too, there were differences. To these we may now turn.

Some terminological complexities must be resolved before we proceed. The concept which is central in the context of aggregation is exchange relation of goods; value is 'exchange value'. Ricardo uses the term value consistently in this sense, and he goes straight into the question of how exchange values are determined in the market. Marx's 'value' is an abstraction; he defines 'value' as equivalent to labour embodied in goods, and reserves the term 'price'

39

to stand for exchange relations, as they are determined in the market. Value is Marx's primary concept, and his problem is why and how far prices deviate from values. Adam Smith also uses the term 'price' as synonymous with exchange value – 'price or exchangeable value' is how he puts it. However, he uses the term 'value' to stand, not for labour embodied in goods, but for labour commanded by goods. It is this latter concept on which, as we have seen, his theory of growth is based. However, it is a concept which is itself to be derived from prices of goods, and these prices, Smith recognizes, need to be explained. In our account of the classical theories of value, we shall fix our attention on the exchange value of goods, or 'relative prices', as they may be called also.

It is sometimes thought that Adam Smith gave several theories of value, not one, and that they are not always consistent with one another.[1] Ricardo, for example, accuses Smith of having 'erected' two labour standards of value, one in terms of the quantity of labour bestowed on the production of goods, and the other in terms of the quantity of labour which it can command in the market, 'as if they are equivalent expressions'.[2] Mention is also often made of Smith's reference to 'toil and trouble', as representing 'what everything really costs to the man who wants to acquire it'. Finally, there is Smith's 'empirical account', as von Wieser describes it,[3] a simple 'cost of production' theory, which runs in terms of various 'components' of price, namely wages, rent and profit.

It is no doubt true that these different concepts are interspersed in Smith's chapters on value. It is also true that later classical economists took over one or the other of these concepts in their analytical framework; Malthus adopts the 'labour command' concept, Senior's 'real cost' has affinity with 'toil and trouble', and Ricardo, as we shall see, adheres to the 'labour embodied' concept, though in a modified form, while J. S. Mill's construction of equilibrium price is based apparently on cost of production. Yet it would be gratuitous to suggest that Adam Smith did not know that they are distinct concepts; also it would be wrong to suggest that, as they appear in Smith's analytical system, they are inconsistent. Let us examine the matter.

[1]See Maurice Dobb, *Political Economy and Capitalism* (George Routledge & Sons, London, 1932), p. 13n; also J. Schumpeter, *History of Economic Analysis* (George Allen & Unwin, London, 1954) p. 188n.
[2]D. Ricardo, *Principles* (Everyman's Library, 1933), p. 7.
[3]F. von Wieser, *Natural Value*, ed. Smart (English translation, Kelly & Millman, New York, 1956) pp. xxvii–xxviii.

The central concept in Smith's system is labour command measure. Chapter V of *The Wealth of Nations*, where Smith introduces the concept of value for the first time, opens with a definition of value which runs in terms of labour commanded. 'The value of any commodity . . . to the person who possesses it, and who means not to use or consume it himself, but to exchange it for other commodities, is equal to the quantity of labour which it enables him to purchase or command. Labour, therefore, is the real measure of the exchangeable value of all commodities.'[4] It is clear that Adam Smith is in search of a measure of value, and he takes labour as the measure. But why labour? Could not any other commodity be chosen as the standard? Smith considers the candidature, in particular, of gold and silver and corn, but he finds that they vary in their value and are sometimes cheaper and sometimes dearer. Labour, too, it is noted, may purchase a greater or less quantity of other goods; but, he argues, 'it is their value which varies, not that of the labour which purchased them'. Labour is supposed to maintain a constant value to the labourer in terms of sacrifice of 'his ease, his liberty and his happiness', in so far as he is 'in his ordinary state of health, strength and spirits' and 'in the ordinary degree of his skill and dexterity'. 'Labour alone', we are told, 'never varying in its own value, is alone the ultimate and real standard by which the value of all commodities can *at all times* and places be estimated and compared'.[5] Clearly labour is adopted as the standard because it is supposed to be invariable with respect to time; the value concept in Smith is linked with his theory of growth, as we saw earlier.[6]

One can now see how the concept of 'toil and trouble' fits into the system. It should be clear that the expression is used by Smith only to elucidate the concept of labour. Apparently, not being satisfied with the representation of a unit of labour in terms of

[4]Adam Smith, *Wealth of Nations*, (Everyman's Library, 1933), vol. I, p. 26.
[5]Ibid., p. 29, emphasis mine.
[6]It is thus misleading to say, as Schumpeter does, that Smith's labour standard is analogous to Walras's *numeraire* (J. Schumpeter, *History*, pp. 188, 310). The concept of *numeraire* in Walrasian economics is just a device for working out determinateness in the system of prices in the context of general equilibrium of exchange. For this purpose any commodity in the circle of exchange could be chosen as the *numeraire* so long as it is applied consistently; there is no special property to be attached to the commodity chosen. Smith's standard, on the other hand, has to be invariable over time. It is a 'measuring rod' to be used for comparing values at different points of time (see A. K. Dasgupta, 'Adam Smith on Value', *The Indian Economic Review* (August 1960), pp. 111–12).

'man-hour', in view of varying degrees of 'hardship endured' and 'ingenuity exercised' in an hour's labour, Smith resorts to what he regards as the subjective counterpart of labour. It is indeed a sort of a footnote. Whether the footnote is at all necessary from the point of view of Smith's value analysis is a separate matter – perhaps it is not. In any event there can be hardly any doubt that Smith did not mean it to be an independent concept; it is obvious that it is ancillary to his basic concept of labour as a standard.

Now, the purchasing power of commodities in terms of labour, which is what 'labour command measure' stands for, is not a *theory* of value; it does not *explain* how exchange value is determined in the market. Nor does Smith intend his labour command measure to serve as a theory. Yet he needs a theory to explain 'exchange value', for otherwise the quantity of labour commanded by the aggregate of commodities cannot be known. It is in this context that he introduces the limiting case of 'an early and rude state of society', where land is not appropriated and capital is not accumulated, where therefore whatever is produced goes to the labouring class. In this simple case, labour commanded by commodities is identical with labour embodied in them, so that the value of commodities, as defined in terms of labour command, can be derived in a straightforward manner from the quantity of labour that is bestowed on their production. 'In this state of things', observes Smith, 'the whole produce of labour belongs to the labourers; and the quantity of labour commonly employed in acquiring or producing a commodity is the only circumstance which can regulate the quantity of labour which it ought commonly to purchase, command, or exchange for.'[7] Here again it is not that the two concepts are unrelated, nor is it that Adam Smith was unaware that they are distinct. In the special circumstances postulated, the two approaches converge, so that the derivation of 'labour command measure' turns out to be simply arithmetic; 'labour cost' is invoked here by Smith to indicate the method of deriving 'labour command measure', not to provide anything like an approach to a theory of value.[8]

---

[7]Adam Smith, *Wealth of Nations*, vol. I, p. 42.
[8]So it is that Schumpeter declares, after examining Smith's various approaches, that 'in spite of his emphasis on labour factor, his theory of value is no labour theory at all'. (J. Schumpeter, *History*, p. 189n.)

Adam Smith

What, then, is Smith's theory of value? How does he *explain* exchange values of commodities?

Let us recall the consideration that is involved in Smith's quest for a theory of value. Now that we are acquainted with his theory of growth, we may start from that end. Smith's growth index, let us remind ourselves, is $\Delta L/L$ – the rate at which employment of productive labour increases over time, which is also, abstracting from the scale effect on labour productivity, an index of the rate at which the wealth of nations grows. The basic variables are W, S, and w; $(L + \Delta L)$ is derived from these variables and is given by $(W + S)/w$. Now, W and w represent bundles of goods which have the same composition; W/w is thus unambiguous. This, incidentally, is why, when S merges into W as in that 'early and rude state of society', there arises no complication. In an 'advanced society', the surplus is appropriated by classes other than the labourers; it thus represents a bundle which does not necessarily consist of wage goods only; it may contain luxury goods of various sorts. In such a state, S is not comparable with w, so that S/w does not convey any precise meaning.

Adam Smith's answer to the problem is that, although the goods as such that comprise surplus are not comparable with the goods that comprise wages, their prices are, that these prices are determined in the market and are expressed in money terms. However, and this is important, it is not the observed prices at any point of time – 'market price', as he calls it – with which Smith is concerned. The price that he considers to be relevant to the measurement of wealth is what he calls 'the natural price' – a central price, towards which market prices gravitate. Smith equates the natural price of a commodity to the sum total of rent, wages and profits that are associated with its production. 'When the price of any commodity is neither more nor less than what is sufficient to pay the rent of the land, the wages of the labour, and profits of the stock employed in raising, preparing, and bringing it to market, according to their natural rates, the commodity is then sold for what may be called its natural price.'[9] Adam Smith's theory of value is, in the ultimate analysis, a cost of production theory. Market prices are freakish and

[9]Adam Smith, *Wealth of Nations*, vol. I, p. 48.

are influenced by accidental circumstances. They are high, or low, according as the amount of a commodity demanded at its cost price – 'effectual demand', as Smith calls it – exceeds, or falls short of, the stock supplied in the market. However, whenever the market price of a commodity deviates from its natural price, forces come into play whereby it is brought back to its natural level; the market price of the commodity reacts on the constituents of its cost of production – rent, wages and profits – and, according as they rise or fall, resources are transferred to or from the industry producing the commodity. 'The quantity of every commodity brought to market naturally suits itself to the effectual demand.'[10] The forces that accomplish this adjustment, Smith urges, are the forces of competition; natural prices of commodities are the resultant of competitive forces operating through the market.

Now, although seemingly innocent, Adam Smith's cost of production theory raises problems of interpretation. Smith takes an individual producer of a commodity, or a trader, 'the person who brings it to the market', as his point of reference to start with. In this context, factor prices are given from outside by the general conditions of the market; and as these are supposed ultimately to be resolvable into rent, wages and profits, there is a case for saying that rent and wages paid out in the process of production and marketing, and profits of the capitalist at the 'ordinary rate' prevailing 'in his neighbourhood' should together set the level to which the price of the commodity must conform, if the business is to run on steadily.[11] Yet even here the question remains as to how the 'ordinary rate' of profits itself is determined. When Smith allows his theory to extend to the aggregate of commodities, the procedure does seem to be open to question; it appears as if Smith argues that rent, wages and profits grow, as distributive shares, out of the prices of the commodities, and at the same time that just these elements, as costs, determine the prices of commodities. This obviously is circular reasoning. It would, however, be unfair to imagine that Adam Smith is capable of committing this simple fallacy. Schumpeter interprets the theory as showing 'the fact of general interdependence between the elements of the economic system', and he goes on to suggest that it constitutes one of Smith's

[10]Ibid., p. 50.
[11]Ibid., p. 49.

'greatest merits in the field of pure analysis'.[12] While one appreciates Schumpeter's anxiety to present Smith as a precursor of Walras, it is doubtful if his interpretation is in accord with the general framework of Smith's system. If what we have learnt about the perspective of his economic theory is correct, then it would seem clear that Smith could not have any concern for a Walras-type functional theory of prices. Smith's quest was for the source of value, and he sought it in factors of production. Let it be remembered that 'value', as Smith defines it, is the measure of wealth, and the sources of wealth are labour, land and capital stock. Costs inhere in these factors, and these determine the value of output. In a society where land is abundant, and capital stock is owned by the labourers themselves, factor costs are unambiguous; the entire output comes back to labour, so the labour commanded by the output turns out to be equal to the labour that is directly employed for its production. The source of value in this simple case can be said to be labour, and labour alone. Where, however, the surplus is separated from wages, the quantity of labour commanded by the output exceeds the quantity of labour bestowed on its production, and the existence of non-labour sources of value becomes revealed. In this advanced state of society, non-labour sources thus come in explicitly as a part of costs with which value is to be equated. How are these costs to be taken into account? Adam Smith seeks a 'par' (as Cantillon would call it)[13] between the various sources, and he finds it in factor prices – rent, wages and profits. Equation between the sum of factor prices and the sum of commodity prices is a truism, and Smith takes it for granted. However, the causal relation that he envisages runs from factor costs to commodity prices.

Now, for the approach to be free of circularity it must explain factor prices independently of commodity prices. This is where Adam Smith falters. He takes care of the rate of wages, as later classical economists do also, be equating it to some kind of a subsistence of the labourers; wages are thus given from outside the price system. Rent is an encumbrance, and Smith seems to be uneasy about it. Rent is seen as forming a part of the cost of bringing a commodity to market in the same sense in which wages and profits

---

[12]J. Schumpeter, *History*, p. 557n.
[13]Richard Cantillon, *Essai sur La Nature Du Commerce En Général*, ed. Henry Higgs (Macmillan, London, 1931), part I, ch. XI.

are. 'In the price of corn, for example, one part pays the landlord, another pays the wages or maintenance of labourers . . . and the third pays the profit of the farmer.'[14] On the other hand, when it comes to the problem of causal relation, rent is shown as price determined, unlike wages and profits. 'Rent . . . enters into the composition of the price of commodities in a different way from wages and profit. High or low wages and profit are the causes of high or low price; high or low rent is the effect of it.'[15] Adam Smith sees monopoly in the ownership of land. Land is limited in quantity, and its owners are supposed to enjoy monopoly power, the extent of which increases as population grows and accumulation proceeds. Rent is thus a monopoly price, and is determined by the tenant's capacity to pay. 'Rent, considered as the price paid for the use of land, is naturally the highest which the tenant can afford to pay in the actual circumstances of the land.'[16] The tenant's capacity to pay is given by the price of commodities on the one hand and the sum of wages and profits on the other. Smith explains the emergence of rent in terms of the productivity of land and the demand for food; demand is sustained by the growth of population, and is supposed, 'in almost any situation', to produce more than is sufficient to maintain, 'in the most liberal way', the labour that is associated with it and also to replace the stock that is employed, 'together with its profits'.[17] The approach seems to come close to the theory of rent which was later to be developed by Ricardo.

How are profits determined? Adam Smith does not have a well-articulated theory of profits either. In the main chapter on profits, there is a suggestion that profits tend to fall as the economy progresses. The tendency, however, is not related to the condition of production; it is ascribed to increasing accumulation and increasing competition among the owners of stock. 'When the stocks of many rich merchants are turned into the same trade, their mutual competition naturally tends to lower profit; and when there is a like increase of stock in all the different trades carried on in the same society, the same competition must produce the same effect in them all.'[18] Profits are thus supposed to be low in opulent societies and

[14]Adam Smith, *Wealth of Nations*, vol. I, p. 44.
[15]Ibid., pp. 132.
[16]Ibid., p. 130.
[17]Ibid., pp. 132–3.
[18]Adam Smith, *Wealth of Nations*, vol. I, p. 78. Once only, as we have noted, does Smith mention diminishing return, and also diminishing profits that result from it; but the matter is not pursued further.

high in poorer ones. Now, this is not a theory of determination of profits; all that it says is that, whatever the rate of profits may be in a given base period, it would tend to fall in a later period in so far as over time the degree of competition increases. We are not told why an increase of accumulation should necessarily be accompanied by an increase in the degree of competition. On what determines profits Adam Smith seems to have little more to say than that the level of profits has a minimum and a maximum. The minimum is set by the subsistence of the person who employs his stock in business. 'As, while he is preparing and bringing the goods to market, he advances to his workmen their wages, or their subsistence, so he advances to himself, in the same manner, his own subsistence which is generally suitable to the profit which he may reasonably expect from the sale of his goods. Unless they yield him this profit, therefore, they do not repay him what they may properly be said to have really cost him.'[19] On the other hand, there is a possible maximum. 'The highest ordinary rate of profit may be such as, in the price of the greater part of commodities, eats up the whole of what should go to the rent of the land, and leaves only what is sufficient to pay the labour of preparing and bringing them to market, according to the lowest rate at which labour can anywhere be paid the bare subsistence of the labourer.'[20] Adam Smith does not have a firm theory of profits; his value theory thus remains incomplete. The theory, however, could be rescued from the vagueness that it apparently has if one were to interpret Smith as saying that there is a conventional rate of profit around for the owners of stock to go by. Perhaps Smith did mean that.

There is a further, more difficult, problem. If our interpretation of Smith's method of defining the relation between factor costs and commodity prices is correct, then it does appear that it does not suffer from the fallacy of circular reasoning of the sort that is commonly attributed to it. It is clearly a one-way relation that Smith contemplates; the relation proceeds from factor costs to commodity prices. Yet, in so far as factor prices are supposed to be determined independently, the procedure finds itself involved in another, more subtle, kind of circularity. While profits, for example, form a share of the output whose 'value' Smith seeks to measure, do they not

[19]Ibid., p. 49.
[20]Ibid., p. 86. As an example Smith cites the case of the East India Company. 'The profits of the trade which the servants of the East India Company carry in Bengal may not perhaps be very far from this highest rate.' (Ibid., p. 87).

affect the value magnitude from which they are supposed to be derived? If they do, are we not led to the odd proposition that the size of the output that is meant to be distributed, as profits and wages, itself changes as the manner of its distribution changes? This is a question which Ricardo raises. Marx's criticism of Smith's method of defining 'sources of value' also derives from this. 'If I determine the lengths of three different straight lines independently, and then form out of these three lines as "component parts" a fourth straight line equal to their sum, it is by no means the same procedure as when I have some given straight line before me and for some purpose divide it, "resolve" it, so to say, into three different parts. In the first case, the length of the line changes throughout with the length of the three lines whose sum it is; in the second case, the length of the three parts of the line are from the outset limited by the fact that they are parts of a line of given length.'[21] This is the kind of ambiguity, Marx complains, which Smith's procedure involves. Smith indeed allows price to 'resolve' into wages, rent, and profits while at the same time seeking the 'sources of value' in just these elements. This requires examination.

The physical output which labour produces with a given amount of land and capital stock is given by the technical condition of production – division of labour, as Adam Smith would put it. Ownership, as such, is irrelevant so far as production is concerned. The fact that in Smith's 'advanced state of society' ownership of resources passes from the labourers to other classes in society should not make any difference to the output. This precisely is why Adam Smith describes rent and profits as 'deductions' from a predetermined output. If in this scheme the 'value' of output, as measured by labour commanded, exceeds the labour embodied in it, it only means that earnings of labour are lower than what they would be in the 'early, rude state of society'. The matter is better seen when a line is drawn in either case at the minimum consumption of the labouring class; for, then, even where ownership vests in labour, the output can be shown to include a surplus. It is just this surplus indeed which is transferred to the landowners and capitalists in the advanced state of society. Marx insists, as does Ricardo, that value analysis must be such as would preserve this structure. If Adam Smith's value analysis fails to do it, it does contradict his 'deduction' theory.

[21]Karl Marx, *Capital* (Foreign Language Publishing House, Moscow, 1957), vol. II, p. 383.

There is no doubt that Adam Smith's value analysis involves a contradiction. Let us examine how. Let us proceed, as before, by assuming that an initial amount of labour L produces an output Q. Let us also assume that w is the minimum consumption rate of the labouring class, which is also the rate of wages. Then, $Q = W + S$, where W is aggregate wages and S is surplus. If labourers accept the minimum standard in any circumstances, then the 'value' of S should be the same whether the surplus is retained by labour or it is transferred to other classes; in either case the quantity of labour which S could accommodate would be the same. Now consider Smith's value analysis as he applies it to the capitalist economy, where indeed it belongs. Let us assume, as we did before, that rent merges into profits. On this assumption $Q = W + P$, profits P being identified with surplus. Put L and m for the quantity of labour that W and P command in the market respectively. Thus, $W/w = L$, and $P/w = m$. Now, $P/wL = r$, or $P/w = rL$, where r stands for the rate of profit. Combining these we have

$$\text{Value of } Q = (W + P)/w = L + m = L + rL = L(1 + r)$$

We are thus led on to the conclusion that the value of output Q is a function of the rate of profits, while the rate of wages remains the same. This of course could not happen if Q were taken as given, as it should be. With Q given, the rate of wages should fall as the rate of profits rises, and vice versa. Failure to show this inverse relationship between wages and profits is a lacuna in Smith's system – a 'ridiculous blunder', as Marx would put it.[22] One conceivable way out of this impasse is to discard the factor-price approach altogether and to reduce costs to one single homogeneous factor. This indeed is the way which Ricardo, and following him Marx, chose to adopt.

David Ricardo

Ricardo's primary concern is with the behaviour of profit in an economy. His theory of growth, as we have seen, is based on the concept of a falling rate of profits. He has thus to define profit properly and to disentangle it from output. If output is represented

[22]Ibid., vol. II, p. 372.

in terms of a single commodity, corn, the process of disentanglement does not involve a standard of measurement. We have seen how Ricardo avoided the problem of the standard in his original exercise on the distribution of income. Rent is separated out with reference to the margin of employment of capital and labour, wages are assumed to be given from outside and profit is defined as what is left over. Further, total profit being known, the rate of profit is derived simply by relating it to the total wages advanced. Thus

$$P = Q - (R + W)$$

and

$$r = P/W$$

where P is total profit, Q is output, R is rent, W is wages and r is the rate of profit.

Now, in the corn model all these entities are homogeneous; the process of subtraction and division that the above equations involve does not therefore cause any trouble. Where, however, the goods that the various entities represent are heterogeneous, they have to be represented in terms of a common standard before one can be subtracted from, or divided by, the other. This is where the problem of value comes in. Ricardo faces the problem when, as in his *Principles*, he proceeds to generalize his theory to cover heterogeneous goods.

Let us remind ourselves that Ricardo does not define value in the abstract. He addresses himself straightaway to the problem of the determination of exchange values, of 'relative prices'. The concept of 'absolute value', such as there is in his system, is itself derived from exchange values. On this there is a sharp difference between Ricardo's system and the system adopted by Smith and Marx. Smith, as we have seen, is in search of a standard in terms of which the 'value' of a single commodity, as also of output as a whole, could be measured. Even where he refers to exchangeable value, or prices, he looks in the first instance for the price of a single commodity and then compares it with the prices of other commodities, money costs being assumed to represent these prices. Marx, on the other hand, equates the 'value' of each commodity to its labour content, and then proceeds to compare the 'value' relations between commodities with their relative prices.

Ricardo's procedure is different. Ricardo rejects Smith's 'cost of production' approach, as also his labour command measure. However, he states his labour theory of value, not in terms of an equation of the value of a commodity, which has an 'absolute' meaning, with its labour content, as does Marx later, but in terms of an equation between the *relative* values of commodities with the *relative* quantities of labour that they contain. 'The value of a commodity, or the quantity of any other commodity for which it will exchange, depends on the relative quantity of labour which is necessary for its production, and not on the greater or less compensation which is paid for that labour.' This is how Ricardo opens his chapter on value. He closes the penultimate section of the chapter with a reinforcement of his theory thus: 'It is necessary for me also to remark that I have not said, because one commodity has so much labour bestowed upon it as will cost £1000, and another so much as will cost £2000, that therefore one would be of the value of £1000, and the other will be of the value of £2000; but I have said that their value will be to each other as two to one, and that in those proportions they will be exchanged. It is of no importance to the truth of this doctrine whether one of these commodities sells for £1100 and the other for £2200, or one for £1500, and the other for £3000; into that question I do not at present inquire; I affirm only that their relative values will be governed by the relative quantities of labour bestowed on their production.'

How is the theory sustained? Ricardo solves the problem by an ingenious model. What, in effect, he does is to reduce the three-factor production structure into a one-factor model. First, he eliminates land by resorting to the concept of a margin of production where no rent is paid. Rent, as we have noted in our corn-model demonstration, is the excess of average product over marginal product. In the marginal product there is no element of rent; the marginal product is to be attributed to labour and capital only. Now, the marginal physical product of a unit of labour and capital is the 'dual' of the marginal cost of a unit of output in terms of labour and capital. In so far, therefore, as product at the margin does not include rent, cost at the margin also does not include land; we are in a region, so to say, where land is free.[23]

---

[23]The assumption that is implicit here is that land is 'specific' to commodities whose exchange values we are in search of. In the context of the value of corn in relation to manufactured goods, which apparently was Ricardo's concern, it is indeed a plausible assumption.

The other simplifying device that Ricardo proposes is to assume that the proportion in which labour and capital are employed in various industries is the same. Capital, says Ricardo, is 'accumulated labour' which the capitalists own and advance towards production. The duration of these advances depend upon the ratio of circulating capital to fixed capital and also upon the durability of fixed capital. If, therefore, the ratio that current labour bears to accumulated labour is the same in all industries, and if the length of time for which the advances are locked is also the same, then the determinant of relative prices is reduced to a single factor, labour. Under free competition the rate of profits, as also the rate of wages, tends to be the same in all industries. Hence, in so far as labour bears a uniform ratio to capital in various industries, relative prices tend to be equal to the relative quantities of labour embodied in them. This is Ricardo's labour theory of value in its pristine form.

On these assumptions, the derivation of the rate of profit becomes as simple as in the corn model. For, now we have an index in terms of which goods comprising profits can be compared with goods comprising wages; the rate of profits can thus be shown as being determined by the ratio of labour embodied in aggregate surplus to labour embodied in wages. To use Piero Sraffa's apt expression, labour, instead of corn, now appears 'on both sides of the account'.[24]

It is a highly simplified model on which Ricardo builds his labour theory of value. Yet, even as it is, the theory brings out an important truth. It demonstrates, in contrast with Smith's doctrine, that a rise in wages does not raise prices; if wages were to rise uniformly in all industries, then, on this model, relative prices of commodities would remain unaffected, only the rate of profits would fall.[25]

However, Ricardo is aware that his labour theory of value is not rigidly true; in reality labour and capital appear in unequal combinations in the production of different commodities, and hence relative prices do deviate from the relative quantities of labour embodied in commodities. Yet, he urges that his labour theory is a good approximation. On the other hand, the error in Smith's

[24]*The Works and Correspondence of David Ricardo*, ed. P. Sraffa (Cambridge University Press, 1951) vol. I, Introduction, p. xxxii.
[25]This inverse relationship between wages and profits comes out clearly in the Ricardian diagram (figure 1). If OW rises, the vertical gap between it and the marginal productivity curve shrinks, and profits fall; nothing happens to rent. This same phenomenon should be reflected in the corresponding cost curve, if they are properly drawn.

theory, he suggests, becomes more glaring when industries use labour and capital in unequal proportions. For, in such cases, contrary to what Adam Smith would have us believe, a rise in wages causes prices of some commodities to fall; in so far as free competition ensures uniformity in the wage rate and the profit rate in different industries, a uniform rise in wages lowers the prices of those commodities in which the ratio of capital to labour is relatively high, while it raises the prices of those in which the ratio of capital to labour is relatively low.

While Ricardo modifies his labour theory of value in view of the diversity in labour–capital configurations in different industries, he is led into a consideration of a standard in terms of which changes in the exchange values of goods could be measured. We have seen that when wages rise, exchange values of goods change; some prices rise and some prices fall. The question, then, arises: in terms of what are these price changes to be indicated? It is a question which marks the transition from exchangeable value to absolute value – from an inquiry into the cause of value to an inquiry into a measure of value. Ricardo's quest for 'an invariable measure of values' proceeds from just this inquiry. 'It is', he declares, 'a great desideratum in Pol. Econ. to have a perfect measure of absolute value in order to be able to ascertain what relation commodities bear to each other at distant periods.'[26] He thus finds himself involved in the problem which Adam Smith had initiated. However, the route that he takes to arrive at this standard is very different from Smith's. While Adam Smith proceeds from the concept of absolute value to exchangeable value, Ricardo proceeds from exchangeable value to absolute value. And having already discovered the 'curious effect' on exchange values of a rise (or fall) in wages, he is careful so to choose his standard that the values of the aggregate product, measured by it, remains independent of the manner of its distribution; Ricardo's invariable standard is to be invariant to changes in wages or profits.

Now, if products are to be attributed to labour alone, the standard is the same as the standard of Smith. Further, if the labour-capital ratio is the same in all industries, exchange values are independent of wages and profits, and any one of the commodities exchanged in the market is capable of being used as a standard; we are virtually on a one-commodity model. Complications arise

[26]D. Ricardo, *Works*, vol. IV, p. 396.

when the labour–capital ratios are different in different industries. For, then, exchange values depend not only upon the relative quantities of labour employed in production but also upon the relative length of time for which 'accumulated labour' is advanced by the capitalist – upon 'labour and profits' as Ricardo (rather awkwardly) puts it. In this situation, which is what the real world provides, the choice of a standard raises difficult issues. First, there is hardly a commodity in the real world which is at all times produced under the same circumstances. If circumstances vary, if the commodity chosen as the standard contains different proportions of labour and capital at different times, it will itself vary in value as wages, or profits, vary. Secondly, even if an unvarying commodity is at all available, the commodities whose values are to be measured may not have the same properties as those of the chosen standard; and if this happens, the measure fails. Measurement implies comparison, and one can only compare like with like. Note the highly suggestive statement of Ricardo: 'This then seems to hold universally true that the commodity valued must be *reduced* to circumstances precisely similar (with respect to time of production) to those of the commodity in which the valuation is made.'[27]

However, while Ricardo is disturbed over these limitations, he yet does not dismiss the concept of an invariable standard. Assuming that in the large majority of cases the limitations do not much matter, he fixes his eyes on an 'average' proportion of labour and time pertaining to the system, and chooses to adopt as his standard a commodity the circumstances of whose production would conform to this average. He believes that such a commodity would agree 'more nearly with the circumstances under which the greater number of commodities are produced than any other which can be proposed'.[28] Within this middle area therefore there is a way of getting at a measure of profit in terms of the standard chosen. The ruling rate of profit in this area is the rate to which, on this assumption, the prices of all commodities in the system would tend

[27]D. Ricardo, *Works*, vo. IV, pp. 386–7. Italics mine. This, it would appear, is the principle which provided the clue to Sraffa's discovery of what he calls the standard system see P. Straffa, *Production of Commodities by Means of Commodities*, (Cambridge University Press, 1960), ch. IV. Here Sraffa demonstrates how it is possible, by using suitable multipliers, to extract out of an actual production structure a system wherein the net output should not only contain the same commodities but also should have the same coefficients as the means of production would – thus satisfying the principle proposed by Ricardo for an invariable standard.

[28]D. Ricardo, *Works*, vol. IV, p. 372.

to be adjusted, so that there may prevail a uniform rate all over. There will be dissimilar commodities on either side of the standard. As wages rise and profits fall, prices of these dissimilar commodities will vary; where the labour–capital ratio is disproportionately high, prices will rise, and where the labour–capital ratio is disproportionately low, prices will fall – all these reckoned with reference to the standard. The point to note, however, is that the average price level will remain the same in terms of the standard.

The difficulty which one is supposed to encounter in finding a general measure of absolute value is on a par with the difficulty that confronts the labour theory of exchange values. In either case the difficulty proceeds precisely from the fact that commodities are produced with unequal combinations of labour and capital. Ricardo perceives the difficulty, indeed he enunciates it in clear terms. No doubt he fails to give an exact solution of the problem. Yet, rather than abandoning the quest, he offers a solution which, as he claims, is 'as near an approximation as can be theoretically conceived'.[29]

Karl Marx

Marx's theory of value is akin to, yet distinct from Ricardo's theory. Marx, like Ricardo, is critical of Smith's approach to value, and he seeks the source of value in factor costs rather than in factor prices. Thus Marx also, like Ricardo, formulates his theory of value in a manner which makes value independent of the manner in which output is distributed. Further, like Ricardo, he lays emphasis on the inverse relationship between wages and profits; indeed recognition of this antithesis figures as one of the salient features in Marx's economics, as it does in Ricardo's.

However, whereas Ricardo begins with the concept of relative prices, as they are determined in the market, and relates them to the labour embodied in commodities, Marx immediately adopts a labour embodied theory of value and asks how and to what extent relative prices deviate from relative values. Marx has two systems – the 'value system' and the 'price' system. Value, represented by labour embodied in commodities, is the essence – the 'inner relation', as he would call it, while price is merely an 'appearance'.

[29]D. Ricardo, *Principles*, p. 28.

Marx does not formulate an independent theory of price; he only shows to what extent prices of commodities, as determined in the market, deviate from their values.[30] The price of a commodity according to Marx, is its 'cost-price' plus the average rate of profit in the economy as a whole.[31] Let it be recalled that Marx defines the rate of profit in terms of surplus value relative to total capital employed, $s/(c+v)$. It is shown that, the rate of exploitation s/v remaining what it is, the rate of profit in an industry would depend upon c, and would be less in those industries where the organic composition (Ricardo's capital-labour ratio) is higher, and more in those where the organic composition is lower, than if relative prices were to conform to relative values. However, since competition in the market tends to equalize the rate of profits in different industries, relative prices tend to be adjusted in such a way that they do deviate from relative values; prices of those commodities tend to be higher than values which have higher than average organic composition of capital, and prices of those commodities tend to be lower than values for which the organic composition of capital is lower than average. Relative prices are supposed to conform to relative values on the special hypothesis, namely that the organic composition is the same in different industries.

How does Marx solve the aggregation problem? There is clearly an aggregation problem in Marx's system, as there is in the system of Adam Smith and Ricardo.[32] Marx does not bring in the problem of aggregation explicitly in his value system. The reason obviously is that in his value system the problem of aggregation is automatically solved. Value in this system is absolute value, measured in terms of labour embodied in commodities. Exchange values thus merge into absolute values. The measure of value is labour embodied in

---

[30]It is this procedure of Marx that drew the sarcastic remark of Paul Samuelson: 'Truth always equals error plus deviation'. *Collected Scientific Papers of Paul Samuelson*, ed. Joseph Stiglitz (Massachusetts Institute of Technology, Massachusetts, 1966), pp. 347–8.

[31]'The price of a commodity, which is equal to its cost price plus the share of the actual average profit on the total capital invested in its production that falls to it in accordance with a condition of turnover, is called its price of production.' Karl Marx, *Capital*, vol. III, p. 156.

[32]M. Morishima argues that Marx was unaware of the problem of aggregation, and he believes that Marx would have elaborated his value theory as an aggregation theory if he had had a chance to read Keynes's *General Theory* (M. Morishima, *Marx's Economics*, (Cambridge University Press, 1973), p. 10. One wonders why Marx should have to be reborn to learn macro-economics from Keynes – he had his predecessors, especially Ricardo, to lean on.

commodities. Thus, in his value system, capital goods as well as consumption goods, including luxuries, are found to be amenable to aggregation in terms of labour. When it comes to the price system, however, the difficulty of aggregation is recognized, in so far as the organic composition of capital is different in different industries. It is this difficulty that leads Marx to his famous disquisition on transformation. The answer that Marx proposes is that while individual prices may deviate from values, the aggregate price tends to conform to the aggregate value. Marx, as we have seen, transforms value into price by adding the average rate of profit to the 'cost-price' of individual commodities, and he argues that since the rate of profit chosen for this transformation is the average rate, the discrepancies between prices and values, in so far as they arise from diversities in the organic composition of capital, would tend to cancel out, so that the aggregate price would turn out to be equivalent to the aggregate value. Thus he says: 'The sum of the prices of all commodities produced in society – the totality of all branches of production – is equal to the sum of their values.'[33]

All this looks very Ricardian indeed; but there are differences, and these differences are vital. First, the value to which Marx seeks to link prices is absolute value, measured in terms of labour embodied, while with Ricardo the price is never equated to its labour content, except in the hypothetical case where there is no capital involved in production. Thus if, in Ricardo's system, the prices of all commodities were to be added in terms of his chosen measure, the aggregate price would turn out to be equal to total labour employed plus profits. Secondly – and this is related to the above – while Ricardo takes as his measure a representative commodity, with an average capital–labour ratio, which itself contains an element of profit, besides labour, Marx fixes his eyes on an average rate of profit. It should be noted however that Marx's profit does not lie outside the labour content of commodities, it is indeed what he calls surplus value. He relates profits to total capital $(c + v)$ which he takes over from his value system.[34] So it is that he finds that,

---

[33]Karl Marx, Capital, vol. III, p. 157. Note that in this exercise Marx explicitly brings in the difference between the total stock of c, which is a base for the calculation of the rate of profit, and the used-up c, which enters into the 'value of commodities' (ibid., table on p. 154). There is an arithmetical slip, surprisingly taken over from the original German edition, in the table (column 4, row 6); the figure should be 22%, not 110%.

[34]M. Morishima rightly points out that the concept of profit belongs to Marx's price system, while the surplus value concept belongs to his value system. However, he seems to be unfair to Paul Sweezy, Joan Robinson and Paul Samuelson, when he complains that in expounding

in the aggregate, price conforms to value. There is evidence that he is aware of the error that is involved in his definition of 'price of production'. 'Since', he cautions, 'the price of production may differ from the value of a commodity, it follows that the cost-price of a commodity containing this price of production of another commodity may also stand above or below that portion of its total value derived from values of the means of production consumed by it.'[35] If indeed he had followed it up, he would have found himself precisely in the world of Ricardo, where 'cost of production' meant 'labour and profits'.[36] If in spite of this, he chose to stick to the labour theory of value in its pristine form, it is because he was anxious to exhibit a rigid link between the rate of profit and the 'rate of exploitation' and thus to lay bare a certain class struggle that is inherent in the capitalist system.

The Upshot

What is the upshot of all this? Ricardo, it will be recalled, claimed, in near desperation at his inability to formulate a precise theory of value, that a theory of profits, and hence a theory of growth, could be worked out independently of value. To what extent is this claim justified? Would, for example, Ricardo's theory of capital accumulation and growth remain valid irrespective of what forces govern output prices? Does the theory survive outside the corn model with which Ricardo starts his enquiry?

Let us note that, in the general case also, Ricardo in his analysis of distribution virtually relied on a one-commodity model. His labour standard is indeed a device to convert the economy into one such model. The limitation of the approach was recognized; indeed, as we have observed, Ricardo was clear about the property of a true standard of value and went so far as to suggest a clue to the

---

Marx's theory they have confused the two systems; the confusion is due to Marx himself, and not due to his critics. See M. Morishima, *Marx's Economics*, pp. 46–7.

[35]Karl Marx, *Capital*, vol. III, 162; also pp. 202–3.

[36]Note, for example, the interpretation of Joan Robinson in this regard: 'The famous argument, that, if one quarter of corn exchanges for x cwt of iron, they must contain the same quantity of labour, can be restated: when there are uniform rates of profits and wages in an economy, these two commodities evidently contain the same quantity of costs of production, composed of wages of the labour, and profit at the ruling rate on the value of capital, directly and indirectly required to produce them.' See 'Value and Price', in *Marx and Contemporary Scientific Thought* (Mouton, The Hague, 1969), p. 334.

determination of such a standard. However, he failed concretely to identify it in terms of any known commodity. He thus fell back in the end on his labour standard, arguing that it was a close approximation to the true standard.[37] We now know, thanks to Sraffa, that one could work out a 'standard system' from a given structure of production, which would satisfy Ricardo's test. However, for applying such a system to the kind of problem which concerned Ricardo, one would have to assume that the technical coefficient of production of commodities in the economy is fixed and constant over time. Ricardo, it will be remembered, does make this assumption concerning the use of capital and labour. In his system, as indeed in the classical system as such, factor proportions are assumed to be independent of factor prices.

In so far as technical coefficients of production are allowed to vary with factor prices, the classical theory of accumulation and growth goes awry. This, as we shall see, is where the marginalists break new ground. In the marginalist system substitution plays a crucial role, and substitution tends to alter technical coefficients of production as factor prices vary. It is not merely that marginalism recognizes factor substitution as a reality; the raison d'être of marginalism rests just on this principle. The concept of margin indeed implies substitutability of commodities in respect of consumption and of factors in respect of production. The procedure however, involves sacrifice of the classical problem. The marginalists, as will be seen, confine themselves basically to a static framework for their analysis of value and distribution; their system fails to deal with accumulation and growth.

If the classical economists allowed themselves to adopt a rough-and-ready measure of value, they did it for a very good reason. For, by so doing, they could enlarge their perspective, as indeed they sought to; the central problem of classical political economy was the problem of accumulation and growth. It is not surprising that modern growth theory, in so far as it derives from Harrod, assumes that relative prices remain constant over time and that if inventions occur they tend to be 'neutral'. It is also not surprising that the theory which proceeds on this assumption tends in the ultimate analysis to be one of a steady state, not different in the essentials from a stationary state of the Ricardian mould.

---

[37]The effect of variation in profit rates on relative prices, Ricardo argues, is 'slight'. See D. Ricardo, *Principles*, p. 22.

5

Theory of Class Conflict

The Concept

What is a class? On what basis did the classical economists divide the society into classes? How do the different classes, as they appear in the classical system, stand in relation to one another and in relation to society? Are these relations one of harmony or one of conflict? These are questions which require to be answered before one can understand the full significance of the classical theory of distribution. They are questions indeed which I have especially emphasized in my definition of classical political economy.

We have seen that the classical economists divide the society into three classes – capitalists (stock owners, or 'masters', as Adam Smith would call them), landowners and labourers. Marx also follows the same classification,[1] although in the central part of his analytical system – the theory of value and the theory of exploitation – he ignores the identity of rent and concentrates on capital–labour relations only, apparently subsuming land under capital.[2] It seems clear that the classification is based on the properties of the factors of production and the functions of their owners. In the economic system which the classical economists take as their frame of reference, capitalists are the dominant class, the class which takes the initiative in production. The capitalists possess resources with which they hire factors of production which the other classes own.

[1]See Karl Marx, *Capital* (Foreign Language Publishing House, Moscow, 1959), vol. III, ch. 52, pp. 862–3. Marx could not finish the chapter. This is a pity; we have been deprived of his interpretation of the tripartite classification which he takes over from Smith and Ricardo.
[2]Paul Sweezy, however, quotes a letter which Marx had written to Engels, saying that in the central part of his work he assumed landed property to be nil. See P. Sweezy, *The Theory of Economic Development* (Dennis Dobson, London, 1946), p. 67. Marx's concern here is indeed to show the mechanism by which a surplus is created and to juxtapose it against wages.

The output of industry belongs in the first instance to the capitalists; out of it they pay rent to the landowners and wages to the labourers. What is left over are the capitalists' profits. Wages tend to be equal to the bare subsistence of labourers; they therefore consume whatever they earn. Rent, however, tends to increase as the economy progresses. The landowners secure a surplus above subsistence. They have thus the means to accumulate. In so far, however, as they do accumulate they become capitalists; rent is transformed via accumulation into capital. All this typifies the working of what one knows to be the capitalist system. One of the things that classical political economy did was indeed to lay bare the social relations that underlie the working of the capitalist mode of production. If the earlier classical economists, particularly Ricardo, brought in the matter purely in the context of economic growth, Mill and Marx put it up as the central part of their social philosophy.

Both land and labour are 'hired' factors, which their owners place at the disposal of the capitalists. However, their economic properties are different, even as their physical properties are. While the supply of land – 'original and indestructible powers of the soil' (as Ricardo defines it) – is fixed and constant, the supply of labour is elastic – indeed perfectly elastic, thanks to peoples' urge to multiply, as Malthus or Ricardo would view it, or to chronic unemployment contrived by the capitalists, as Marx would have it. Within each class the members have an identity of interest. The classical economists take an aggregative view of the economy; they ignore conditions in individual industries and concentrate on the 'general level' of wages, rent or profits. The problem that interested them is, as we have seen, the progress of wealth in the economy and its distribution among classes – each taken as a whole.[3]

How the capitalist class got possession of the resources with which they direct production is history. Neither Smith nor Ricardo cared to go into this history. Ricardo took the capitalist system as he found it, a system in which private property is allowed by the state and in which labourers, not having any material resources in their possession sell their labour in the market against wages. A part of the surplus over wage costs goes as rent to the class who owns

[3]This reminder seems necessary because in later developments of economic theory – in the micro system, that is – one is confronted with a criticism of Marx's theory of class conflict, which runs in terms of a possible conflict of interest also among different groups of labourers. See, e.g., Lionel Robbins, *The Economic Basis of Class Conflict* (Macmillan, London, 1939), ch. 1, especially sect. 5.

property in land; a part remains with the capitalists for them to consume and to accumulate. What is saved (the wages fund) is spent on additional productive labour; capitalists transform their savings into capital. Accumulation is indeed defined by Ricardo, as by Smith, as the process of transforming savings into capital, or in other words, of using what is saved for the employment of productive labour.[4]

Adam Smith no doubt looks back to a rude state of society where land had not yet been appropriated, and capital had not been accumulated. Yet he also considers accumulation as a spontaneous process, antecedent to division of labour and exchange,[5] which the capitalist class initiates, and possession of private property in land as a spontaneous act of appropriation which the state legitimates.

Karl Marx, on the other hand, ascribes the origin of accumulation ('primitive accumulation', as he calls it) to 'force'. He traces it to the expropriation of the agricultural producers and the creation of a body of landless proletarians. 'In the history of primitive accumulation, all revolutions are epoch making that act as levers for the capitalist class in course of formation; but above all, those moments when great masses of men are suddenly and forcibly torn from their means of subsistence, and hurled as free and unattached proletarians on the labour market.'[6] Marx cites the example of England where it had 'the classic form'. Of the immediate followers of Ricardo, John Stuart Mill had a similar view concerning the origin of accumulation. Thus he says: 'The social arrangements of modern Europe commenced from a distribution of property which was the result, not of just partition, or acquisition of industry, but of conquest and violence.'[7] Mill did not go as far as Karl Marx in his reaction against the capitalist system; he did not predict a drastic collapse of the system, as did Marx. Yet he, alone among the direct followers of Ricardo, showed misgivings about its future in a manner which comes close to Marx's prognosis. On value and distribution Mill follows Ricardo. His analysis of class relations is also Ricardian; but his perception of the implications of these relations is distinct

---

[4]'When we say that revenue is saved and added to capital, what we mean is, that the portion of revenue, so said to be added to capital, is consumed by productive, instead of unproductive labourers.' D. Ricardo, *Principles* (Everyman's Library, 1933), p. 94n.
[5]'Accumulation of stock must, in the nature of things, be previous to the division of labour.' Adam Smith, *Wealth of Nations* (Everyman's Library, 1933), vol. I, pp. 241–2.
[6]Karl Marx, *Capital* (Foreign Languages Publishing House, Moscow, 1958), vol. I, p. 716.
[7]J. S. Mill, *Principles of Political Economy*, ed. W. J. Ashley, Longmans, London, 1920, p. 208.

from that of any of his predecessors. Since it comes close to the socialists, we take up Mill and Marx together separately. In the following two sections we discuss how Smith and Ricardo viewed the problem.

Nature of Class Conflict

Referring to Adam Smith's system of political economy, Gunnar Myrdal observes: 'A sunny optimism radiates from Smith's writings. He had no keen sense for social disharmonies, for interest conflicts. . . . On the whole, it is true to say that he was blind to social conflicts.'[8] The pronouncement is difficult to explain. Let us remember that it is Adam Smith who declared that rent and profits are 'deductions' from the produce of labour, that landlords 'love to reap where they never sowed', and that profits of stock 'bear no proportion to the quantity, the hardship, or the ingenuity of the capitalist's labour of inspection and direction'. The author of these propositions cannot surely be said to have been oblivious of class conflict in a capitalist economy. Myrdal, one is afraid, read too much into Smith's concept of the 'invisible hand'. An individual pursues his own gain, but in doing so, he is 'led by an invisible hand, to promote an end which was no part of his intention'[9] – this is Adam Smith's celebrated dictum, and it certainly suggests optimism. Smith, however, intended the dictum to apply, as the context shows, to allocation of resources, not by any means to distribution of income among classes. In the latter context he said things which, far from being optimistic in their implications, rather provided ammunition to socialists. In the system of political economy that Adam Smith built, class conflicts play an important part; and it is this system that gave direction to the thinking of the other members of the classical school.

The problem of class relations is seen by classical economists from a static as well as a dynamic point of view. In its static aspect the problem is one of the sharing of a *given* output among the different classes. Adam Smith offers a bargain theory, suggesting how the labouring class is at a disadvantage in the sharing of the fruit of

[8]G. Myrdal, *The Political Element in the Development of Economic Theory* (English translation, Paul Streeten, Routledge & Kegan Paul, London, 1953), p. 107.
[9]Adam Smith, *Wealth of Nations*, vol. I, p. 400.

its labour. He argues that the capitalists, by virtue of the ownership of stocks, succeed in bringing down wages to bare subsistence. Smith wrote at a time when there were laws preventing combination. The laws covered both the workers and the masters. In practice, however, they applied especially to workers. The masters could take concerted action surreptitiously, while the workers would find it difficult to combine without being detected. Even where workers could combine, they had weaker bargaining power, for they could not hold out as long as the masters could. 'What are common wages of labour, depends everywhere upon the contract usually made between those two parties whose interests are by no means the same. The workers desire to get as much, the masters to give as little as possible. The former are disposed to combine in order to raise, the latter in order to lower the wages of labour. It is not, however, difficult to foresee which of the two parties must, upon all ordinary occasions, have the advantage in the dispute, and force the other into compliance with their terms. The masters being few in number, can combine more easily . . . [and] can hold out longer.'[10] The class that owns capital thus acquires power over workers and can control the labour market to its advantage. Similarly it is ownership of land that gives the landlord title to rent. The title is legal, the result of a specific institutional arrangement; it is not ethical, Smith would surely say, for the landlord reaps 'where he never sowed'.

Ricardo's demonstration of capital–labour relationship is more general and analytically more rigorous. Whereas Smith leans on capitalists' combination to explain conflict, Ricardo demonstrates that there is in general an inverse relation between wages and profits. So long as the technique of production (in other words, the ratio in which labour and capital are combined in production) is given, a higher (or lower) rate of wages is shown by Ricardo to be invariably associated with a lower (or higher) rate of profits. The proposition, let us remember, comes out in the context of the theory of wage–price relationship which Ricardo formulates in opposition to Smith. High wages, he says, do not mean high prices; where, for example, the proportion of labour to capital used in different industries is the same, higher or lower wages leave prices of commodities unaltered, while compensation comes from an opposite movement in profits. Higher rate of wages thus means lower rate of profits and not higher prices. This inverse relation between wages and

[10]Ibid., pp. 58–9.

profits, it will also be remembered, is more readily seen in the one-sector model of Ricardo. If, on the diagram (figure 1), which we have used in the context of Ricardo's theory of distribution, OW shifts upwards, or in other words, if for any level of employment (of labour or capital, for the two are used in a fixed proportion), the wage rate becomes higher, then the rate of profits necessarily becomes lower. There is thus an inherent conflict between labour and capital in the sharing of output.

There is also a dynamic aspect, where the problem relates to the sharing of a *growing* output consequent on accumulation and division of labour. This part of the analysis brings to light not merely conflicts of interest between classes as such but also the way in which these interests are related to the general interest of the society. Ricardo's theory of distribution, in particular, is largely an analysis of this problem. The propositions, as set out in the one-sector corn model of Ricardo, have been noted in an earlier chapter. As accumulation proceeds and employment of more labour accompanies it, aggregate output grows, but it grows at a diminishing rate, so that with given technology and with a constant rate of wage, rent rises and profits fall, both as a share of output and per unit of capital. In a bi-sector model also, the same relation obtains, except that now the shares are measured in value terms; the phenomenon of diminishing returns in agriculture is reflected in higher value of goods which the labourers consume, so that wage per unit of labour tends to rise in value terms, which industry has to bear. However, the rate of profits, being a ratio between output and input, both measured in terms of the same standard, behaves as in the corn model; it tends to fall. Hence the famous Ricardian proposition concerning the effect of progress on distribution: rent rises, wages rise and profits fall. Nevertheless, the wage rise being only in value terms and not in real terms, the condition of labour remains the same, and the conflict turns out to be essentially between the landowners and the capitalists.

Adam Smith had given a similar theory. In his system, too, as accumulation proceeds and the economy grows, there is a natural tendency of profits to fall, of rent to rise and of wages also to rise. However, the resemblance between Smith's theory and that of Ricardo is only superficial. The difference between the two is fundamental. In Ricardo's system rent rises and profits fall on account of the niggardliness of nature. Accumulation intensifies it, and the conflict between capitalists and landlords grows. The repeal of the Corn Laws, controversy over which was the occasion for the Ricardian theory of rent and profits, would injure the landowners but benefit the capitalists. The interest of the landlords in the Ricardian system is thus opposed to the interest of the society, whereas the interest of capitalists conforms to the interest of the society – higher profits being conducive to accumulation and growth. Smith, on the other hand, is led by his theory to identify the interest of the landlords with the interest of the society, while he regards the tendency to a falling rate of profits as the outcome of increasing competition and hence a welcome phenomenon. On wages also the two systems differ materially. In Ricardo's system wages rise in value terms only, not in real terms. Smith, on the other hand, allows wages to rise in real terms.

These differences are to be explained largely in terms of the discovery of the scarcity theory of rent. Partly also they are due to the fact that whereas Ricardo assumes given technology, Smith allows division of labour to accompany accumulation. Thus, according to Adam Smith, a rise in rent is due to improvement in agriculture associated with progress. Ricardo, on the other hand, would explain it in terms of diminishing return from land; improvements in agriculture would, under Ricardo's theory, lower rent.[11] In the same way, the rise in wages in Ricardo's system is due to an increase in the value of wage goods, consequent on the operation of diminishing return. Smith, on the other hand, defines a 'progressive state' as one in which accumulation and division of labour move ahead of population, resulting in a rise in real wages.

There is, however, one aspect of Ricardo's analysis in this context which carries implications of a conflict specifically between capital and labour. There is no doubt that Ricardo's main concern was with the division of 'net revenue'. His *Essay on Profits* was devoted essentially to this question. As wages were supposed to be but the maintenance cost of labour, wage cost could be regarded as on a par with the depreciation of capital. Net revenue (surplus over the maintenance cost of labour) was thus considered to be the entity whose distribution was relevant to the growth of the economy; the larger the proportion of it that went to the capitalists as profit, the higher would be the rate of growth. Now, while considering the

---

[11]In the short run, but not in the long. The short run, however, is supposed not to be very short. 'A considerable period', Ricardo maintains, 'will have elapsed with a positive diminution of rent'. See D. Ricardo, *Principles*, p. 42.

effect of machinery, he discovered that inventions leading to the use of machinery benefit the capitalists, while they not infrequently injure the labouring class. While investments towards the creation of fixed capital, which is what introduction of 'improved' machinery implies, increase the 'net revenue' of the society, of which profits are a part, they would, at any rate in the short run, reduce the 'gross revenue' out of which wages are paid. Thus he says: 'The opinion entertained by the labouring class, that the employment of machinery is frequently detrimental to their interest, is not founded on prejudice and error but is conformable to the correct principle of political economy.'[12] Capitalists introduce machinery in their own interest, but by so doing they injure the labouring class; the introduction of machinery, Ricardo argues, reduces the wage fund (in the short run at any rate) and hence it either lowers the wage rate or creates unemployment.

Classical Liberalism

Let it be understood that, when Adam Smith identifies the interest of landlords with the interest of the society, what he means simply is that the factor which makes for the progress of an economy, namely accumulation, tends at the same time to raise rent and hence benefit the landowning class. Ricardo also arrives at the same conclusion, though by a different route. Neither of them, however, has any fancy for the landlord class; neither offers the proposition as a justification of higher rent. Rather the contrary. Both show a sense of unease at the prospect that they envisage – Adam Smith, because the landlords reap the benefit without effort, Ricardo because higher rent is at the expense of profit and is therefore a hindrance to growth. On the other hand, both Smith and Ricardo are distressed at the misery of the labouring class, their low bargaining power and their inability to share the fruit of economic progress. Their solicitude for the labouring class is clear. Labourers, Smith argues, 'make up the far greater part of every political society. What improves the circumstances of the greater part can never be regarded as an inconveniency to the whole.'[13] Similarly, Ricardo counts himself as one of the 'friends of humanity' who 'cannot but

[12]Ibid. p. 267.
[13]Adam Smith, *Wealth of Nations*, vol. I, p. 70.

wish that in all countries the labouring class should have a taste for comforts and enjoyments, and that they should be stimulated by all legal means in their exertions to procure them.'[14]

Now, in the face of all this how does one explain the social philosophy of these early classical economists? Why should Smith and Ricardo have accepted an economic system which inevitably results in class conflict, such as their theory of distribution reveals? And having accepted the system how do they meet the dilemma? How, in other words, do they reconcile their theory of class conflict with the policy of economic liberalism – the policy, that is, of free trade and free enterprise?[15] Or do they at all?

Smith advocated free trade because lifting of restrictions on trade would widen the market and would offer greater scope for division of labour. His advocacy of free enterprise is to be explained by his belief that a free scope for the play of profit motive would lead to technological progress. Capitalism was accepted by Smith because he believed it was efficient.

There are, however, one or two things involved in Smith's advocacy of economic liberalism which need elucidation. The system of capitalism that Smith welcomes is *competitive* capitalism, a system which permits free competition among capitalists. Capitalists no doubt have an urge to combine in order to be able to lower wages, or to raise prices, but they also compete among themselves by introducing cost-reducing methods of production. It is such competition, a free exercise of the competitive spirit, that Smith has in mind when he talks of free enterprise. Classical liberalism is indeed based on this concept of free competition; it is, in consonance with the method of the classics, essentially a dynamic concept.[16] Efficiency in Smith's system is also to be understood

[14]D. Ricardo, *Principles*, p. 57.

[15]I take it that this is what constitutes the economic side of liberalism. I would avoid the word 'non-intervention' in this context; non-intervention is a misleading word, though often used, to describe classical liberalism. Smith and his followers gave very much a positive role to the state. The state, under Smith's system, is not merely to maintain the internal and external security of the country: its 'third and last duty . . . is that of erecting and maintaining those public institutions and those public works, which, though they may be in the highest degree advantageous to a great society, are, however, of such a nature that profit could never repay the expense to any individual and small number of individuals and which it therefore cannot be expected that any individual or small number of individuals should erect or maintain', (Adam Smith, *Wealth of Nations*, vol. II, pp. 210–11). There is no evidence that later classics denied this principle.

[16]We shall notice in the next chapter that this concept is very different from the concept of 'perfect competition' which Cournot introduced in economic literature and which the later marginalists adopted.

primarily in the dynamic context; free enterprise, as Smith sees it, releases forces which make for division of labour and is therefore conducive to economic progress. It is technological efficiency (as one may call it) in which Smith is primarily interested.[17]

Thus, while recognizing the distributional anomalies that inhere in the capitalist system, Smith yet hoped that under a system of free trade and free enterprise, technology would improve and the condition of the labouring class would gradually improve, and that free competition among capitalists would tend to reduce profits to a socially permissible level. Landlords' rent, though an evil (except when it is accumulated), is accepted as a necessary concomitant of progress.

Ricardo's system does not offer any such saving features; the condition of the labouring class remains depressed in spite of accumulation and progress. Profits tend to fall, and they fall not on account of increasing competition among capitalists, but on account of nature's resistance to progress. Rent has a tendency to rise, unless checked by improvements in the method of agriculture and unless such improvements are continuous (or at least frequent); improvements lower rent only in the short period. If, in spite of all this, Ricardo accepted the capitalist system, the reason simply is that he took the system as he found it, and made it his task to analyse its features and examine wherein its strength or weakness lay. His findings no doubt carried revolutionary implications, but he himself remained a liberal. He fought for the abolition of the Corn Laws because it would, in the specific case of his own country, lower the price of corn, lower wages in value terms and raise profits at the expense of rent. On the same ground he was opposed to the prevailing Poor Laws. These laws, he argued, were a tax on accumulation of the rich, while they only added to the number of the poor – 'instead of making the poor rich, they are calculated to make the rich poor'.[18]

---

[17]This is not to say that Adam Smith ignored allocational efficiency altogether. He did not. The celebrated 'invisible hand' is supposed to see to it that capital is employed in industries which realize a relatively higher exchangeable value to the capitalist and hence a relatively higher revenue to the society. Smith uses the argument in the specific context of the employment of capital in domestic industry as against foreign industry, although he would surely wish us to recognize its wider applicability. What is important, however, is to remember that here also, having argued that an individual who employs his capital prefers domestic industry to foreign industry, having regard to security, Smith hastens to add that the individual 'endeavours so to *direct that industry* that its produce may be of the greatest possible value'. Adam Smith, *Wealth of Nations* (Everyman's edn), vol. I, pp. 399–400. Italics mine.
[18]D. Ricardo, *Principles*, p. 61.

Ricardo's acquiescence to private property and private enterprise is based on his belief that these institutions stimulate accumulation and enterprise. His chief interest lay in the maintenance of profit which, as he saw, was the sole source of accumulation and growth. It is not true, as is often alleged, that he was a biased apologist for the capitalist class. His concern was for the economic progress of the society, and he just found that the interest of the capitalist class coincided with this objective. It is not true either that he was apathetic to the labouring class. Here also his theory of population, which he took over from Malthus, led him to the conclusion that the remedy for the deprivation of the labouring class lay in a restriction in their numbers. 'It is a truth which admits not a doubt that the comforts and well being of the poor cannot be permanently secured without some regard on their part, or some effort on the part of the legislature, to regulate the increase of their numbers, and to render less frequent among them early and improvident marriages'.[19]

Both Smith and Ricardo saw deficiencies in the institution of capitalism. Both recognized disharmony in class relations, and the deprivation of workers which the system entails; but they sought remedies within the system. Smith believed that a free play of competitive forces in the economy would encourage accumulation and division of labour and, in so far as these would go ahead of the growth of population, there would be a gradual improvement in the condition of labour. Ricardo was also anxious to see the condition of labour improve, and would surely welcome continuous innovations for keeping up wages. He was, however, less optimistic about such possibilities. There was the spectre of a stationary state before him, which he viewed with abhorrence. He thus favoured a policy which would maintain intact the source of accumulation while urging the workers to restrict their numbers and to push up their supply price, so that the stationary state, if it came, might be less dismal.

Mill and Marx

We have observed that John Stuart Mill, like Karl Marx, held that the institution of private property was the result of conquest and

[19]Ibid., p. 61.

violence. It is not surprising therefore that he should have refused to maintain an attitude of neutrality to the institution in the manner Ricardo could. Mill, like Marx, derived his theory of value essentially from Ricardo, though unlike Marx who took over the labour-embodied theory in its pristine form, he adopted its amended form to cover time. When it comes to distribution, however, he makes explicit mention of the fact that the division of social output into wages, rent and profits depends upon the kind of institution which the society chooses to adopt. 'The laws and conditions of production of wealth', Mill says, 'partake of the character of physical truths. . . . It is not so with the Distribution of wealth. That is a matter of human institutions only'.[20] Costs and surplus are categories which can be identified purely in terms of the technical conditions of production. In so far as production yields an output which more than covers the subsistence of labour, the problem of an institutional arrangement comes in, for the society has to decide to whom the surplus should go. If, as it happens, a part of it goes to the landlords as rent and a part goes to capitalists as profit, it is because society has adopted an institution – the institution of capitalism – which permits it. Mill asks if there is any inevitability about the institution. For Smith or for Ricardo perhaps it was premature to ask the question.[21] For Mill it was time; the first flush of enthusiasm for economic progress that the industrial revolution had released was over, and Mill found himself in the midst of schemes of institutional rearrangement to improve the system of distribution. He could not help reacting to his environment. He thus made it his special concern to consider economic theory overtly with reference to its application to social philosophy.[22]

Mill's position in regard to the choice of a social institution is one of ambivalence. He definitely rejects the state of capitalism, as he found it. If the choice were between socialism 'with all its chances' and capitalism as he found it in practice with its 'sufferings and injustices' then of course he would opt for socialism. But he saw possibilities of improvement of society even within the structure

[20] J. S. Mill, *Principles of Political Economy*, pp. 199–200.
[21] It is interesting to note that Marx recognized this. For, witness his observations on Ricardo's concern for production of wealth. 'Ricardo, rightly for his time, regards the capitalist mode of production as the most advantageous for the creation of wealth. He wants *production for the sake of production* and this with *good reason*' (Karl Marx, *Theories of Surplus Value* (Foreign Languages Publishing House, 1968)), vol. II, p. 117. Italics mine.
[22] The title of his book is explicit on this.

of capitalism. Two conditions, he proposed, were essential for the success of any scheme of social improvement: limitation of the number of population and universal education. Granted these conditions, he would leave it to 'futurity' to determine where comparative advantage lay in terms of 'human liberty and spontaneity'.

This, however, is not all. Mill made a conjecture as to what futurity would be like for the labouring class. The conjecture apparently was based on his intense awareness of the growing strength of this class. In Ricardo's time labour was still passive; Mill saw unions gathering strength.[23]

Mill's analysis of class relations is distinct in its boldness of perception. While it derives from the 'bargain' theory of Adam Smith, it takes account of the possibilities of labour, too, as a social force. Mill does not believe in the continuance of any class other than labour, and if he still chose to recognize the labouring class as distinct from a capitalist class, it was 'as description of an existing, but by no means a necessary or permanent, state of social relations'. The existence of a non-labouring class is a 'great social evil, which can be accepted only provisionally'. Thus he says: 'I do not recognise as either just or salutary, a state of society in which there is any "class" which is not labouring; any human beings, exempt from bearing their share of the necessary labours of human life, except those unable to labour, or who have fairly earned rest by previous toil'.[24] However, he goes on to argue, so long as a labouring class exists, as it does, and is dependent for employment and wages upon a class of employers, there will be conflict between the employer and the employed, and the conflict will grow as labourers become more and more aware of their rights and privileges. The situation is unsatisfactory not only to the employees but also to the employers. 'If the rich regard the poor, as by a kind of natural law, their servants and dependents, the rich in their turn are regarded as a mere prey and pasture for the poor, the subject of demands and expectations wholly indefinite, increasing in extent with every concession made to them.' Such a relation could not be sustained for long. Unlike his

---

[23]Combination Acts were repealed in 1824, a year after the death of Ricardo. Trade union activity started soon after, even though in a sporadic manner. By the middle of the forties it had assumed enough importance to catch discerning eyes.

[24]This, and the quotations that follow in this and in the following paragraph are taken from J. S. Mill, *Principles of Political Economy*, book IV, ch. VII. One must read this magnificent chapter if one wishes to get the nuance of Mill's theory of class relations.

predecessors, Mill asks what the probable long-run consequence of the conflict would be, and his conjecture is that the employing class would in the end give in.[25]

Mill considers, as an alternative, the theory of 'dependence and protection', then in vogue in certain quarters, under which the employers should be benevolent guardians of the employed, looking after their interest with the care of a protector, and the employed would give 'good work for good wages' – the relation between the two being one of 'affectionate tutelage on the one side, respectful and grateful deference on the other'. In spite of the 'seductive' picture that it conveys of the future society, he rejects the theory, for it is unreal and belongs to 'a rude and imperfect state of social union'. Where, as in advanced societies, the ordinary working men were taught to read and had access to newspapers, where they were brought in numbers together to work under the same roof, were given political power through electoral franchise, and above all where 'dissenting preachers were suffered to go among them and appeal to their faculties and feeling in opposition to the creeds professed and countenanced by their superiors', there the theory of dependence and protection would be untenable; 'long before the superior classes could be sufficiently improved to govern in the tutelary manner supposed, the inferior class would be too much improved to be so governed'. Mill, on the other hand, envisages a state of 'self-dependence' on the part of the labouring class – a gradual supersession of the existing relation by 'partnership', initially in the form of association of labourers with capitalists, and finally 'perhaps' in the form of association of labourers among themselves.

Mill had thus a vision of a classless society. It is not clear, though, how sanguine he was about its arrival. It was a 'probable' future that he contemplated. Even as he contemplated it, however, the transition was to be gentle. For the workers' awareness of their rights and also their competence to stand by themselves would, as he saw

[25]Mill, it may be noted here, took over what is known as the 'wage fund' theory from Smith and Ricardo – a theory which proposes that there is a predetermined fund for distribution as wages to the labourers, its magnitude depending upon the decision of the capitalists as to what proportion of profits they would accumulate. He then argued that trade unions could not raise the rate of wage beyond what is warranted by the wage fund. Later, under pressure from friends he recanted it and conceded that the fund had an elasticity which permitted a leeway for trade union manoeuvring. However, while agreeing that the fund to be expended on labourers was elastic, he yet argued that 'there is an impassable limit to the amount which can be so expended'. One would think Mill has this limit in his mind when he envisages the possibility of the employer giving in.

it, come in the wake of universal education, although the process might be aided by the appeal of 'dissenting preachers'.

It was Karl Marx who turned the theory of class conflict into a revolutionary channel. Marx had before him Adam Smith's explanation of rent and profit as 'deductions' from the produce of labour, and Ricardo's demonstration of a wage–profit antithesis. Weaving these into a theory of exploitation, he sought to show that the institution of capitalism round which classical political economy grew carried with it germs of its own destruction.

We saw earlier that Marx had a value system and a price system and that in the context of the totality of the economy he saw a fair degree of correspondence between the two. In the value system, value of output is by definition equal to its labour content, and wages are equal to the labour content of goods that are necessary for the maintenance of labour. In so far, therefore, as the capitalists get out of the workers an output which is more than is necessary for their maintenance, a surplus arises. This surplus relative to the wages of labour is shown as the measure of the rate of exploitation. It is also shown that the rate of exploitation, as thus measured, is necessarily higher than the rate of profit. In the value system, this follows as a matter of definition; s/v is necessarily higher than $s/(c+v)$. The proposition holds good also in the price system, in so far as it conforms to the value system, as it is supposed to do in the context of the aggregate of commodities. Marx thus concludes that the existence of a positive rate of profit in the market is evidence of a positive rate of exploitation. Further, since the rate of exploitation moves in the same direction as the rate of profit, it is inversely related to the rate of wages, even as the rate of profit is. The capitalists endeavour to maintain as high a rate of exploitation as possible, and they do it by bringing the rate of wages down to the level of minimum subsistence.[26] Thus it is that the 'price' of labour (the wage rate) in the market tends to conform to the 'value' of labour.

Now, this state of things, Marx argues, cannot endure long. Combining the concept of exploitation with this theory of crisis,

[26]This is what Marx calls the 'coercive power of capital'. One notices a family resemblance between this Marxian concept and Smith's proposition concerning profit–wage relationship discussed earlier. Marx does not recognize combination of capitalists, as Smith does; in Marx's system there is 'free competition' among capitalists. Yet there is little doubt that there is implicit in the system an element of monopsony, in that his system allows an individual capitalist to influence wages in the labour market.

he writes a kind of an *ex ante* history, saying that in the process of capitalist exploitation forces are released which tend inevitably to a shift of power from capital to labour. As crises deepen with recurring rounds of booms and slumps, there ensues a struggle between capitalists themselves for the maintenance of profit. There is thus a tendency to monopolization, one capitalist laying 'a number of capitalists low'. In the process, technology improves resulting in increases in the scale of production, while capitalists become fewer in number. Side by side with this development, and as a result of it, there is also a tendency to the assembling of workers under a common organization – 'socialization of labour', as Marx puts it, thus making it possible for them to unite and to fight exploitation. The stage is thus set for the struggle of many against a few. In the struggle the workers win and snatch power from the capitalist class.[27]

John Stuart Mill's *Principles* came out in 1848, the year in which the *Communist Manifesto*, of which Karl Marx was a co-author, was issued. Mill and Marx had thus the same kind of environment to react to. No wonder therefore that the questions to which they addressed themselves were similar. Both saw contradiction in the existing class relations and predicted change. Both envisaged the emergence of a system in which the employer–employee relation would be non-existent. Yet they differed vitally in their prognostications concerning the manner in which the ultimate goal would be reached; whereas Marx, as is well known, believed that the passage would be marked by a violent rupture, Mill's guess was that it would be a gradual transition.

Soon after Karl Marx, however, economic theory found itself shifted to an altogether different channel – away from an analysis of the relation between classes to an analysis of the relation between goods. The marginalists not only introduced a new technique of economic analysis, they also in the wake of it gave a new orientation to the purpose and content of economic theory. The new system, as one looks at it, was a challenge to classical political economy; it thus constitutes our second epoch. To this system, then, we now turn.

[27]See Karl Marx, *Capital*, vol. I, pp. 761–2.

6
Marginalist Challenge

Characteristics of Marginalist Economics

'Economic analysis, serving for two centuries to win an understanding of the Nature and Causes of the Wealth of Nations, has been fobbed off with another bride – a Theory of Value.' This is how Joan Robinson opens the Preface to her *Accumulation of Capital*. The marginalists, she complains, drove economic science into a system of 'arid formalism' and turned it away from problems 'that are actually interesting'. Nicholas Kaldor goes further. Looking for 'Where Economic Theory Went Wrong', Kaldor finds it in Adam Smith's *Wealth of Nations*, chapter IV, where Smith brings in the theory of value. While the earlier chapters offer 'significant' propositions concerning division of labour, in the middle of chapter IV 'Smith suddenly gets fascinated by the distinction between money price, real price and exchange value, and from then on, hey presto, his interest gets bogged down in the question of how values and prices for products and factors are determined.'[1] This Smithian diversion, Kaldor complains, is 'where economic theory went astray'.

These comments are no doubt exaggerated; a theory of value, as we have seen, was not altogether irrelevant to classical political economy. Yet they can be understood, if viewed as a reaction against the ascendency of a system of economics which was to suppress the great questions on growth and distribution, with which the classical economists were chiefly concerned. The new system – marginalism – came as a challenge to classical political economy.[2] It diverted

---

[1] Nicholas Kaldor, 'The Irrelevance of Equilibrium Economics', *Economic Journal*, December, 1972, pp. 1240–1.

[2] In the case of Jevons it was a sort of revolt – witness the manner in which he denounces the Ricardian system: '. . . that able but wrong-headed man, David Ricardo, shunted the car of Economic science on to a wrong line – a line on which it was further urged towards

economic theory away from the mainstream, as it was then, and concentrated exclusively on value and resource allocation. So pronounced was the deviation that with the emergence of marginalism the problems that evoked classical political economy came very nearly to be forgotten.

The marginalist epoch, as we understand it here, begins with the publication of W. S. Jevons's *Theory of Political Economy* and Carl Menger's *Grundsatze*, and ends with Keynes's *General Theory*; the period covered is thus 1871-1936. This specific periodization is important. Marginalism as a technique of economic analysis has had ramifications in several directions in later years. Even Keynes is formally a marginalist, and in recent years many of the propositions of classical political economy, such as, for example, wage-profit relation, are being subjected to scrutiny in terms of the marginalist technique. Since, however, my purpose in the present study is to focus on the specific character of the marginalist challenge as it was thrown up by the pioneers of the system, I leave out later developments.

The advent of marginalism marks a decisive shift in the nature of economic theory. Economic theory ceases to be an enquiry into the causes and implications of the growth of wealth; it becomes an enquiry into the problem of allocation of *given* resources among competing lines of production. Jevons, one of the founders of the new system, puts the matter in clear terms: 'The problem of economics', he says, 'may be stated thus: *Given a certain population, with various goods and other sources of materials: required, the mode of employing their labour which will maximise the utility of the produce'.*[3] This Jevonian formulation sets the tone of economics over the entire epoch; for over sixty years since Jevons wrote, economic theory continued to be viewed chiefly as an enquiry into the conditions of maximization under given constraints.

It should be noted at once that the manner in which the problem is posed makes for a significant shift in the method of analysis. The classical system is directed to an analysis of a 'sequence in time'; the method is 'dynamic', in the sense that the sequence analysed is *irreversible*. In Marx the linking of one period with another in the sequence is explicit, not only in terms of the behaviour of surplus

---

confusion by his equally able and wrong-headed admirer, John Stuart Mill' (W. S. Jevons, *The Theory of Political Economy*, 4th edition (Macmillan, London, 1911), p. li).
[3] Ibid., p. 267.

but also in terms of the services of fixed capital. Smith and Ricardo no doubt worked primarily with circulating capital, so that in their systems the periods analysed seem to be self-contained. Yet the procedure does have a dynamic character in that there is linking of one period with another through the behaviour of profits and of population. The marginalists, on the other hand, employ what is called the 'static' method. The economy is assumed to be stationary by hypothesis. It is assumed, in particular, that the number and character of population remain constant over time, that there is no change in technology nor in the degree of scarcity of resources, and, further, that the tastes of consumers remain unchanged. The method permits variations of proportions; marginalist economics has its basis in the principle of substitution – a principle of which there is no counterpart in classical political economy. Whether it is production or exchange, the relations that the marginalist system incorporates are seen as the outcome of a process of substitution. In the field of consumption it recognizes substitutability between one bundle of goods and another, and in the field of production it recognizes substitutability between one combination of factors and another. The analysis runs in terms of alternative possibilities for the economic subjects to choose from. The method enjoins, it is important to note, that the alternatives are 'open' alternatives and that decisions taken on them are *reversible*. Walras's 'crying of prices' and Edgeworth's 'recontract' are examples *par excellence* of the marginalist procedure.[4] In so far

4Walras's exposition of the mechanism is worth repeating. For exchange equilibrium Walras relies simply on auctioneering. 'When a price is cried and the effective demand and offer corresponding to this price are not equal, another price is cried for which there is another corresponding effective demand and offer.' And so on, until there is equilibrium. In production he recognizes the complication which arises from the fact that services are to be transformed into products. After certain prices of services are cried and certain quantities of products have been manufactured, if these prices and products are not equilibrium prices and quantities, it will be necessary not only to cry new prices but also to manufacture. Walras devised an ingenious method. He imagines, 'on the one hand, that entrepreneurs use *tickets* to represent the successive quantities of *products* which are first determined at random and then increased or decreased according as there is an excess of selling price over cost of production or vice versa, until selling price and cost of production are equal; and, on the other hand, that landowners, workers and capitalists also use *tickets* to represent the successive quantities of *services* at prices first cried at random and then raised or lowered according as there is an excess of demand over offer and vice versa, until the two become equal' (L. Walras, *Elements of Pure Economics*, tr. William Jaffé (George Allen & Unwin, London, 1954), p. 242. See also F. Y. Edgeworth, *Mathematical Psychics* (1881) (LSE reprint, 1932, p. 17). Whether the mechanism contemplated is realistic or not is not the question. The point to note is that the static method which the marginalists employ excludes any *actual* transactions at disequilibrium prices.

as alternatives remain open, decisions of economic subjects, either as consumer or as producer, are experimental (and hence reversible). The process of substitution is thus allowed to persist until, *given* the resources of the economy and, let us add, *given* the distribution of assets, market operations yield maximum product for producers and maximum utility for consumers. The position thus established is deemed to be a position of equilibrium.

Does not the theory of value, one may ask, provide a link between the two systems of economic theory? There are historians who believe that it does. No less an authority than Joseph Schumpeter holds the view that, despite seeming contrasts in approaches, there is essentially a continuity in the development of economic science. 'Thus our science does not lack an organic development. Grown out of the instinctive knowledge of the basic facts of economic life it consolidated itself in connection with the ideas that were formed by the practical experience of the eighteenth century'.[5] This is what Schumpeter says, winding up his discourse on the place of marginal utility in the development of economic science. Now, in so far as the marginalist approach is interpreted merely as a tool of economic analysis in general, as the modern economists would have us do,[6] one may perhaps see a point in Schumpeter's view. But if one does, one misses the real content of marginalism as it emanated from its founders. What, then, are the characteristics of marginalist economics, which distinguish it from classical political economy?

First, while in marginalist economics relative prices form the centre-piece, being the regulator of resource allocation, in classical political economy they have only a subsidiary role. It is true that there is an allocative aspect implicit in the concept of 'natural price' and of a uniform rate of profit, which the classical economists – from Smith to Marx – adopted. Smith's theory of natural price is indeed often cited as a precursor of the marginalist theory of resource allocation. Yet, if our analysis of the classical theories of value is correct, it would seem clear that 'natural price' comes in as incidental to Smith's concept of a labour command measure. Indeed the theory of exchange value figures in classical political economy essentially as a vehicle for a passage to one of absolute value. Classical economists needed a *measure* of value, an 'invariable

---

[5]See J. Schumpeter, *Economic Doctrines and Method*, tr. R. Aris (George Allen & Unwin, London 1954), p. 201.
[6]See, e.g., P. A. Samuelson, *Foundations of Economic Analysis* (Harvard University Press, Cambridge, Massachusetts, 1947), chs 1–3.

standard', in terms of which heterogeneous commodities which constitute wealth could be brought into relation with one another for purposes of aggregation. The marginalist economists, on the other hand, dismiss aggregation altogether as a non-problem. 'The summation of exchange values', says Allyn Young, 'is akin in principle to an attempt to determine the weight of the solar system'.[7] The marginalists analyse relative prices within a static framework, and their concern is with micro-entities – with individual commodities which are assumed to be homogeneous. The classical concept of an invariable standard thus gives way in marginalist economics to the concept of *numeraire*.

Secondly, consumption, not accumulation, appears in marginalist economics as the mainspring of economic activity. The new system, so to say, substitutes 'consumers' sovereignty' for 'capitalists' sovereignty'. Thus the phenomenon of demand, whose place in economic theory the Political Economy Club had once seriously called in question, comes to occupy the pride of place in the marginalist system. Now, this shift of approach has important implications. Once you take accumulation as the motive force behind economic activity, as the classical economists do, you at once recognize the existence of a capitalist class who, by virtue of their ownership of capital, enjoys the privilege of employing labour. The purpose of economic activity is then seen to be to earn profit by keeping the level of wages down to the minimum possible. On the other hand, if consumption is accepted as the motive force, the purpose of economic activity turns out to be the satisfaction of human wants. In one view the end of production is the creation of profit, in the other it is the creation of utility. Profit in classical political economy is derived from given technical conditions of production; in so far as the capital–labour ratio used in production is given, and the wage rate is given, one knows what the rate of profit is. In marginalist economics profit, as it is defined, as also wages, is derived from the sale of commodities.

Thus, thirdly, the theory of distribution assumes altogether a different complexion in marginalist economics. The marginalist system considers distribution as a species of value – a problem of factor prices rather than one of class relations. Unlike classical political economy which derives distribution from the structure of

---

[7]Allyn Young, *Economic Problems New and Old* (Houghton Miffton Co., Boston, Mass., 1927), ch. X, p. 204.

production, the marginalists derive distribution, as they define it, from commodity prices. Carl Menger classifies goods in the order of their distance from final consumption; goods of higher orders – 'factors of production', as he defines them – are supposed to derive value from the value of consumption goods.[8] Distribution is thus conceived as a structure of imputed values. Similarly costs of production are no longer to be treated in absolute terms, as in classical political economy; they are defined in relative terms as foregone alternatives. The term value remains. But the concept is given a distinct slant by the marginalists; it inherits little from the classical system.[9]

Value

The origin of the concept of margin is said to be due to the riddle which Adam Smith posed but did not care to solve, concerning 'value in use' and 'value in exchange'. Smith cites the example of water and diamond, saying that while water has high value in use, it has scarcely any value in exchange, while diamond has high value in exchange but scarcely any value in use. 'The things which have the greatest value in use have frequently little or no value in exchange; and, on the contrary, those which have the greatest value in exchange have frequently little or no value in use.'[10] Smith, however, immediately dismisses the concept of value in use and concentrates on value in exchange. He takes care to define the object

[8]Not only capital but also land and labour are represented by Menger as goods. 'Land occupies no exceptional place among goods. If it is used for consumption purposes (ornamental gardens, hunting grounds, etc.), it is a good of the first order. If it is used for production of other goods, it is like many others, a good of higher order.' So are labour services reckoned as a good of the first order when they yield direct satisfaction, or as a good of higher order when they yield satisfaction indirectly (see Carl Menger, *Principles of Economics*, tr. James Dingwall and Bent F. Hoselitz (The Free Press, Glencoe, Illinois, 1950), pp. 165–73).

[9]If all this is granted, then the term 'neo-classical', which is commonly used to represent the economics of the marginalist school, would surely be misleading.

[10]Adam Smith, *Wealth of Nations* (Everyman's Library, 1933), vol. I, p. 25. The latter part of the statement should not be taken too literally; Smith's intention obviously was to emphasize a contrast. Or, as J. S. Mill seems to suggest, Smith might be using the term 'value-in-use' in a normative sense (J. S. Mill, *Principles of Political Economy*, ed. W. J. Ashley Longmans, London, 1920, book III, ch. I, sect. 2). Ricardo is more cautious in the matter. While he cites examples similar to Smith's to show the contrast between the concepts – water and air on the one hand and gold on the other – he merely says that gold is of little use *compared with* air or water, even though it 'exchanges for a great quantity of other goods' (see D. Ricardo, *Principles* (Everyman's Library, 1933), p. 5).

of his enquiry to be 'to investigate the principles which regulate the exchangeable value of commodities'. Later classical economists follow this lead. Utility, no doubt, finds recognition in their system as a property of commodities, but it is ruled out as a determinant of value. 'Utility', says Ricardo, 'is not the measure of exchangeable value, although it is absolutely essential to it'.[11]

The marginalist technique provides a solution to the Smithian riddle. At the margin there is no contradiction between value in use and value in exchange. Exchange values of commodities conform to their respective 'marginal utility';[12] the 'total utility' of the available quantity is irrelevant to it.

Utility is a subjective concept. The marginalist theory of consumption and value thus takes the individual as its point of reference. In the Mengerian system this is explicit. Menger indeed makes it clear at the very beginning of his chapter on the theory of value that it is the utility for goods on the part of the individual that finds expression in the market. 'Goods always have value *to* certain economizing individuals and this value is also determined only by these individuals.'[13] Jevons no doubt has the concept of a 'trading body', which he employs directly in his theory of exchange. Yet he recognizes the limitations of the concept, suggesting that the so-called trading body represents the behaviour of an average individual; it is a 'fictitious mean', as he calls it.[14]

With given income, an individual consumer equates the price with his marginal utility. By so doing he secures maximum utility out of his income. Market demand is a reflection of such maximizing behaviour of individual consumers. Thus each point on the demand curve represents a position of maximum utility for the consumers constituting the market. Likewise, in the sphere of production, a firm is the point of reference. Given the prices of resources, a firm chooses a technique which minimizes cost; under appropriate assumptions, the minimum cost (including normal profit) is shown to be the same for all the competing firms in an industry. The market

---

[11]D. Ricardo, *Principles*, p. 5.
[12]This particular expression was used first by Philip Wicksteed, as a rendering of von Wieser's 'grenznutzen' (see Alfred Marshall, *Principles of Economics*, Variorum edn, vol. 1, Macmillan, London, 1961) p. 93n). This reminder seems necessary because Keynes in his classic memorial of Alfred Marshall (*Memorials of Alfred Marshall*, ed. A. C. Pigou (Macmillan, London, 1925), p. 22n) attributed the term 'grenznutzen', wrongly as it appears, to Menger, and the adoption of the term 'marginal utility' to Marshall.
[13]Carl Menger, *Principles of Economics*, (English translation, Illinois, 1950), p. 146.
[14]See W. S. Jevons, *The Theory of Political Economy*, pp. 88–90.

supply curve thus represents points of minimum cost (or maximum product) in relation to the employment of resources. A consumer is supposed to vary the proportion in the bundle of goods that he chooses until he secures maximum utility out of his income. A firm is supposed to vary the proportion of different kinds of resources until the cost of a given output is minimized. The entire procedure is worked out in terms of what is called the principle of substitution.

Factor prices, in the marginalist system, are determined in the same manner as prices of commodities. The total supply of factors is assumed to be given; the problem is one of their allocation in different industries. Thus, even as commodity prices are determined as a result of the push and pull of consumers operating on given supplies, factor prices are determined by the push and pull of the users of productive services, and these users are none other than the producers of commodities. In the Walrasian system all these prices are determined simultaneously. Both commodity prices and factor prices derive from the fact of scarcity; commodities are scarce because the resources which are required to bring them into being are themselves scarce. In the Austrian system the factor market is overtly separated from the commodity market, factor prices being conceived as 'imputed values'. The primary force operates on the commodity market, deriving from the felt need of consumers. Commodities command prices because their supply is scarce in relation to the total demand; price in one sense thus measures the strength of the top demand that is excluded. The demand for factors is an indirect demand and is derived from the demand for commodities. The same theory of 'excluded demand' informs factor prices; the price of a factor in any line of production, as von Wieser would put it, measures the strength of the next best alternative to which it could be applied.

Because Walras set up his theory of general equilibrium in terms of simultaneous equations involving both commodities and factors, his approach is often called the 'functional' approach, as distinct from what is called the 'causal–genetic' approach of the Austrians.[15] The characterization does not seem to be meaningful. Both trace the origin of value to utility emanating from the needs of the economic subject; Walras's *rareté* is indeed another name for marginal utility. Walras himself acknowledges it; *rareté* is

[15]See, e.g., Maurice Dobb, *Theories of Value and Distribution Since Adam Smith* (Cambridge University Press, Cambridge, 1973), p. 210.

defined by Walras as a 'derivative of effective utility with respect to the quantity possessed'.[16]

Now this is a matter of major significance. Marginalism is not a mere technique of analysis. As a technique indeed it fits the earlier approach also – is not the Ricardian theory of rent an application of the marginalist technique? If marginalist economics is a challenge to classical political economy, as indeed it is, the challenge consists in the fact that it throws up an alternative to the classical approach to value. In classical political economy the central problem is one of production; labour is here supposed to act on material resources, including land, in order to produce commodities. The basic attribute which gives value to commodities is thus supposed to be labour; commodities possess value because they need, for their production, the application of human labour to resources which are given to society by nature; economic activity is supposed to be a struggle of man against nature. The corollary of this approach, let us remind ourselves, is the recognition of surplus as a category over and above the maintenance cost of labour, and of conflict concerning the disposition of this surplus. Marginalist economics shifts the approach, as we have seen, from production to consumption. The central problem in this approach concerns the wants of consumers. Demand is here supposed to be the primary force from which all economic activity proceeds. So complete is the supremacy of demand in the new system that, in some representations of it, supply figures only as the reservation demand of the sellers of commodities, and when account is taken of production, by the reservation demand of the sellers of factors.[17] The allocation of resources is supposed to be based on the principle of opportunity costs, these costs being considered to be a reflection of the reservation demand for factors of production.

Now the demand for commodities is an expression of a certain behaviour of consumers, market behaviour, as one would say; consumers offer money which they hold in order to buy commodities which they need. It is a behaviour which shows itself in the

---

[16]See L. Walras, *Elements of Pure Economics*, 4th edition (George Allen & Unwin, London, 1954) p. 146. This is also evident from Walras's acknowledgement of Gossen's priority with respect to the formulation of the utility curve and of Jevons's priority with respect to the equation of maximum utility in exchange. L. Walras, *Elements of Pure Economics*, p. 37. Walras thus claims to be one of the founders of the marginal utility principle along with Gossen and Jevons.

[17]See Philip Wicksteed, *Commonsense of Political Economy*, ed. Lionel Robbins (George Routledge & Sons, London, 1934), vol. II, pp. 772–96.

operations of the market. The behaviour needs to be explained; the market relations need to be traced to something which lies outside these relations. This, at any rate, is how the founders of marginalist economics, including Walras, viewed the problem. If classical economists sought the ultimate explanation of value in labour, the marginalists sought it in utility.

Jevons and Menger overtly adopt marginal utility as the explanation of exchange relations. In Walras's system the concept remains suppressed under a set of simultaneous equations. Yet it is very much there to define the degree of scarcity ('constraints', that is) upon which the equations rest. The cause of value is attributed, in the ultimate analysis, to utility in Walras's system, even as it is done in the systems of Menger or Jevons.

There is a certain basic difference between the labour approach and the utility approach, which may as well be stated here. Labour, in so far as it is defined in terms of man-hour, is a concrete entity, whereas utility is not. Labour as a quantity can be perceived directly; whether the labour costs of commodities correspond to their prices or not can be tested empirically. Utility, on the other hand, resides in the minds of individuals; its association with prices is only a hypothesis. It is indeed a hypothesis, not verifiable, that prices of commodities correspond to their relative marginal utility. Although, therefore, utility can be plausibly offered as a property of value, it hardly lends itself to treatment as a determinant of value. One does not proceed from a knowledge of relative utility to prices of commodities. The procedure seems to be the other way about; when one knows relative prices, one hypothesizes that they represent the relative marginal utility of commodities. The theory of utility maximization, which is the keynote of marginalist economics, is a deduction from this hypothesis – undoubtedly a valid deduction, given the hypothesis.

Distribution

While marginal utility as an explanation of value is a common feature of the marginalist system, not all marginalists subscribe to the marginal productivity theory of distribution. The early Walras, for example, proceeds with the assumption of fixed coefficients of production. So does von Wieser, who goes out of his way to criticize Menger's 'Loss Principle' of factor price determination. Menger's principle is essentially a marginal productivity principle, even though it is stated in a manner which lacks precision.[18] Jevons no doubt has an idea of marginal productivity; his concept of 'final rate of production' which he applies to increments in the employment of labour upon a given piece of land is another name for marginal productivity.[19] Jevons's suggestion of a parallelism between the theories of rent and wages indeed carries the germ of a marginal productivity approach.[20] Jevons, however, did not elaborate his thesis. Nor did Walras in the earlier editions of his *Elements*, even though he noted this parallelism; his exercise in marginal productivity theory as such is a later insertion. The marginal productivity theory in its present form appears in the works of J. B. Clark and Philip Wicksteed.

Around the 1880s J. B. Clark formulated a theory of distribution along marginalist lines in a series of articles which were later consolidated in his famous *Distribution of Wealth*.[21] Clark's representation runs in terms of two factors – labour and capital.[22] The analysis is conducted on a diagram, on the lines of the Ricardian

---

[18]This is how Menger defines his Loss Principle: 'The value of a given quantity of a particular good of higher order is not equal to the importance of the satisfaction that depends on the whole product it helps to produce but is equal merely to the importance of the satisfactions provided for by the portion of the product that would remain unproduced if we were not in a position to command the given quantity of the good of higher order' (Carl Menger, *Principles*, p. 164). Menger would have arrived at a proper marginal productivity theory if he had specified the magnitude of the difference between the quantities commanded of the good of higher order, showing that at the margin the loss of product on account of the withdrawal of a unit of the good is approximately equal to the gain in product on account of an addition of a unit. It is because von Wieser failed to recognize the marginal order of this difference that he found fault with Menger's theory, arguing – wrongly, as the marginalists would say – that according to the latter's formula, the sum of factor prices would exceed the total product. Wieser's own representation is based on differences in the proportion of factors used in different industries, even though the proportion in any individual industry is assumed to be fixed. The set of equations by which he solves the problem is the following:

$$x + y = 100$$
$$2x + 3z = 290$$
$$4y + 5z = 590$$

Whence, $x = 40$, $y = 60$ and $z = 70$ (see F. von Wieser, *Natural Value*, tr. C. A. Malloch, Kelly & Millman, New York, 1956, p. 88). Note that the proportions in which the factors x, y and z are used in the three industries are different.

[19]W. S. Jevons, *Theory*, p. 217.

[20]Ibid., Preface to the Second Edition, p.l.

[21]See J. B. Clark, *Distribution of Wealth* (Macmillan, New York, 1927), Preface, pp. V–VI.

[22]Capital, in Clark's representation, stands for 'the whole permanent fund of productive wealth', including land, (ibid., p. 190).

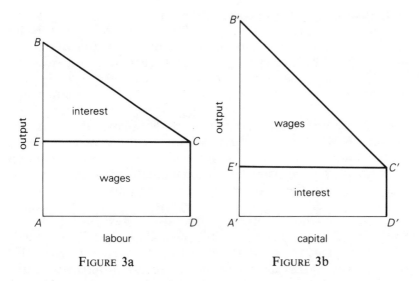

FIGURE 3a   FIGURE 3b

theory of rent, showing interest or wages as the surplus according as capital or labour is assumed to be the 'constant' factor. The demonstration is as follows.

Production takes place with a quantity of labour AD, as shown in figure 3a, and a quantity of capital $A'D'$, as shown in figure 3b. When, as in figure 3a, capital is held constant and labour is 'dosed', interest appears as a surplus. On the other hand when, as in figure 3b, labour is held constant, and capital is 'dosed', wages appear as a surplus.

The marginal productivity curves in both the cases are downward sloping, showing diminishing returns from individual factors of production. In figure 3a, BC represents the marginal productivity (Clark calls it 'final productivity', evidently in deference to Jevons) in respect of labour, so that $AECD$ measures wages and BEC measures interest. In figure 3b, $B'C'$ represents the marginal productivity in respect of capital, so that $A'E'C'D'$ measures interest and $B'E'C'$ measures wages. Clark, then, argues that under static conditions $AECD$ is equal to $B'E'C'$, and $A'E'C'D'$ is equal to BEC; in other words, $AECD$ plus $A'E'C'D$ is equal to $BADC$, or $B'A'D'C'$. Thus when an entrepreneur hires both labour and capital for employment in his undertaking, and wages and interest are paid according to the principle of marginal productivity, the sum of these payments just exhausts the total product of the undertaking. Under 'free competition' the entrepreneur receives no 'profit' – no surplus, that is, beyond the remuneration that is due to his own labour or capital which he may be employing in the undertaking. For, as Clark argues, the presence of profit anywhere 'would be a universal invitation to capitalists to become *entrepreneurs* and, as such, to bid against each other for labour and capital till the profit should everywhere vanish, by being made over to labourers and capitalists in the shape of wages and interest.'[23] What applies to an individual entrepreneur applies to the economy as a whole; in so far as the total output of industry is distributed between labour and capital according to their respective marginal productivity, there remains no surplus.

This is the famous 'adding-up' theorem, which had once eluded von Wieser. Clark limits his analysis to two factors, being handicapped by the plane geometric method that he employs. Philip Wicksteed generalizes the theorem by introducing a production function which takes account of the existence of different categories of labour and capital, and also of different categories of land.[24] Wicksteed discards the 'crude division' of factors into land, capital and labour. He splits up factors into minute categories, such that each factor could be expressed in its own unit. 'We must regard every kind and quality of labour that can be distinguished from other kinds and qualities as a separate factor; and in the same way every kind of land will be taken as a separate factor. Still more important is it to insist that instead of speaking of so many £ worth of capital we shall speak of so many ploughs, so many tons of manure, and so many horses, or foot-pounds of "power" '.[25] Thus, $A, B, C, \ldots$ are supposed to be the factors of production, each of them discrete and homogeneous, and P the product. The production function is then defined as $P = f(A, B, C \ldots)$. It is further assumed that the

[23]Ibid., p. 291n.
[24]Wicksteed's treatment of the problem is to be found in his *Coordination of the Laws of Distribution* (1894) (LSE, reprint, 1934) sect. 6.
[25]Ibid., p. 33. Delinking of 'factors' from 'classes' is thus complete. Wicksteed seems confident that the classification of factors into discrete categories would not affect the viability of the marginal productivity concept; he believes that, within limits, all factors are substitutable, in the sense that the use of any of them can be economized, if need be, in favour of others. 'And yet, within limits, the most apparently unlike of these factors of production can be substituted for each other at the margins, and so brought to a common measure of marginal serviceableness – in production. Thus though no amount of intelligence or industry can make bricks without straw, yet intelligence may economise straw, and one man with more intelligence and less straw may produce as good bricks as another with more straw and less intelligence.' (P. Wicksteed, *Commonsense of Political Economy*, vol. I, p. 361.)

production function is of the form, such that if $P=f(A,B,C\ldots)$, then $mP=f(mA, mB, mC\ldots)$, for all (positive) values of m. It then follows, from the rules of partial differentiation, that

$$\frac{dP}{dA}A + \frac{dP}{dB}B + \frac{dP}{dC}C + \ldots = P$$

This means, in economic terms, that the product equals the quantities of the various factors multiplied by their respective marginal productivities. The condition that makes for the validity of the theorem, as revealed by the form of the production function, is that there should be constant returns to scale. In Clark's model also, the marginal productivity of labour or capital is deduced by varying their proportions, and is assumed to be independent of the scale of production. What, however, is implicit in Clark's model is here explicit. Wicksteed explicitly assumes constant returns, and is at pains to show how it is a valid assumption, not only in physical terms but also, in so far as perfect competition prevails in the market, in value terms.

Once, however, the assumption of constant return to scale comes out explicitly, a further question arises. Is constant return to scale compatible with perfect competition? Would a firm find equilibrium if, while its average cost remains constant, it takes the price as given in the market? Would it not expand output indefinitely until it comes to a position from where it could influence the price of its product in the market and, perhaps also, the prices of factors of production? And once an element of monopoly creeps in, the adding-up theorem breaks down, as Wicksteed himself recognizes.[26] The contradiction in Wicksteed's solution was detected soon after it arrived. Walras's entry into the marginal productivity area is indeed due to his reaction to Wicksteed's formulation of the 'adding-up' theorem. Walras, and also Wicksell independently, discovered the lacuna in Wicksteed's solution. They proposed an amendment to the proposition, saying that, while constant return to scale is a sufficient condition of the validity of the theorem, it is not a necessary condition; all that is necessary for its validity is that there should be a 'minimum cost' point on the average cost curve of a firm. A firm, they argued, could well operate under increasing return over a certain range, and yet,

---

[26]P. Wicksteed, *Coordination*, p. 38, where Wicksteed repudiates 'any commanding presumption that industries concentrated in a few hands come under this law'.

in so far as it faces diminishing return at some stage, there must be a critical point which exhibits the property of constant return. Wicksteed's solution is shown to be valid in so far as the firm finds equilibrium at this minimum cost point.

This, however, is not the end of the story. As it transpires, for the Walras–Wicksell postulate to be valid, there has to be one factor associated with the firm which is indivisible; and for it to be consistent with the adding-up theorem, the indivisible factor has to be of an order such that, even though it is optimally exploited, the size of the firm to which it belongs remains within the limit which is compatible with perfect competition in the industry. These are highly restrictive conditions to which reality would almost certainly refuse to conform. This, however, is a different matter. For our purpose the point especially to note is that the marginal productivity theorists endeavoured to establish not only that their theory is self-consistent, but also, as a corollary, that the owner of a factor employed in production, be it capital or labour, gets a return which is just equal to its economic contribution (as one may call it) to the social product, leaving no surplus.

Why Marginalist Economics?

Clearly, then, marginalist economics stands substantially apart from classical political economy. The marginalists pose new questions and devise new modes of answering even old questions. Not only is a new technique introduced into economic analysis, but the structure and content of economic theory also receives a new orientation.

Why did this happen? What could be the urge behind this drastic shift of approach?

There are technical reasons no doubt. The classical theory of value and distribution had deficiencies which called for rectification. The labour theory could not be accepted as a general theory of prices. It does not cover cases – rare pictures for example – where prices have little relevance to the labour involved in production. Even where labour does appear as a significant factor of production, relative prices of goods fail to conform to their relative labour costs when labour–capital ratios are different in different productive processes. Thirdly, labour itself is not a homogeneous category – indeed it grew to be less so with the increasing mechanization of industry and the development of varieties of skill. A unit of labour could thus hardly be defined in unambiguous terms. These are obvious deficiencies; but there are others which are not so obvious. The labour theory fails to explain prices of goods which have joint costs; you cannot identify the specific cost of individual commodities when they are produced jointly in the same process of production. On the other hand, labour cost becomes ambiguous in those cases where alternative techniques are available within the same technology for the production of commodity. In the former case the number of productive processes is less than the number of prices to be determined. In the latter case the position is reversed; the number of processes is greater than the number of prices to be determined. In either case the labour cost of a commodity is indeterminate.[27]

The deficiency that pertains to the theory of distribution appears to be more fundamental. Once the hypothesis that wages are physiologically determined at a subsistence level is rejected, the classical theory breaks down altogether. This precisely is the point that Jevons makes in his critique of Ricardo's theory of distribution. Jevons accepts the Ricardian proposition that at the margin rent is zero. Yet, as he argues, there are two unknown quantities still to be determined, and Ricardo is left with the 'simple equation', produce = profit + wages. Jevons dismisses Ricardo's theory of distribution, arguing that it involves an attempt to determine two unknown quantities from one equation. 'Something might perhaps be made of this doctrine if Ricardo's theory of a natural rate of wages, that which is just sufficient to support the labourer, held true. But I altogether question the existence of any such rate'.[28] Much the same stricture applies to Marx's theory of distribution, even though the route by which Marx arrives at his wage theory is different from Ricardo's route. Ricardo leans on the Malthusian theory of population, while Marx invokes the 'coercive power of capital', to explain why wages tend to sink to the level of workers' subsistence. The proposition could not of course be considered valid in the context of an economy where labour had become scarce. The matter becomes more complicated when it is recognized that it is not one wage rate, but a multiplicity of wage rates, as Wicksteed reminds us, that need to be brought under the principle of distribution.

[27]See on this, Michio Morishima, *Marx's Economics* (Cambridge University Press, 1973), ch. 14, pp. 179–80.
[28]W. S. Jevons, *Theory*, p. 269. Walras also makes the same kind of argument in his critique of the 'English' theory of distribution. See L. Walras, *Elements*, lesson 40, p. 425.

It is not as if the classical economists were unaware of these deficiencies. 'Rare pictures' is Ricardo's example.[29] It is Ricardo again who underlines 'the difficulty of comparing an hour's or a day's labour in one employment with the same duration of labour in another'.[30] The complication due to unequal labour–capital ratios in industries is of course a major problem that troubled both Ricardo and Marx. In regard to the theory of distribution also, both Ricardo and Marx knew that there is no rigid subsistence to which wages could be related. Ricardo would argue, as he does indeed, that subsistence is not a rigid concept, that it varies with the level of a country's development. In Marx's system the determination of wage–profit ratio is a matter of class struggle; it thus leaves scope for a deviation of wages from subsistence. The crucial hypothesis in both is that wages are determined from outside and are therefore given.

In any event, the hypothesis that the classical economists made served them well enough, considering the purpose of economic theory that they had in view. Indeed, at the time when they wrote, their assumptions could be taken as a fair approximation to reality. In the early years of the industrial revolution, when classical political economy grew, labour was abundant and its bargaining power was low. Varieties of skill were yet to assume significance. Techniques of production could be taken to be more or less constant and independent of factor prices; Ricardo's construct of a 'unit of labour and capital', implying constancy in the labour–capital ratio, was not altogether a fanciful construct.[31] Joint production could be treated, as indeed John Stuart Mill did for example, as a 'peculiar' case of value.[32] Commodities like 'rare statues and pictures' could of course be left aside as irrelevant.

[29]'There are some commodities' Ricardo observes, while introducing his theory of value, 'the value of which is determined by scarcity alone . . . Some rare statues and pictures, scarce books and coins, wines of a peculiar quality, which can be made only from grapes grown on a particular soil, of which there is a very limited quantity, are all of this description. Their value is wholly independent of the quantity of labour originally necessary to produce them, and varies with the varying wealth and inclinations of those who are desirous to possess them.' D. Ricardo, *Principles*, p. 6.
Considering the import of this passage, and having regard to the fact that Ricardo had a notion of 'margin' implicit in his formulation of the theory of rent, one may well wonder if he could not have, had he so wished, given us a marginal utility theory of value.
[30]Ibid., p. 11.
[31]Note that this was an indispensable construct for Ricardo. For once he allowed capital–labour ratio to vary with a falling profit rate relative to wages, his theory of accumulation would break down.
[32]J. S. Mill, *Principles*, book III, ch. xvi. The chapter is titled, 'Of Some Peculiar Cases of Value'; joint production is cited as one of the peculiar cases.

Over the half-century after Ricardo, thanks to the growth of industrialization and innovations, conditions changed drastically in the economies of the West, especially England, the home of classical political economy. Labour became scarce, and the subsistence theory became outdated. Innovations led to the emergence of alternative techniques of production in industries and along with them, different varieties of skill. Thus factor proportions could no longer be assumed to be independent of factor prices, and existence of different kinds of labour had to be explicitly recognized in the analytical system. Marginalist economics may be said to be the outcome of a recognition of these events. The marginal productivity theory of distribution indeed rests on recognition of factor substitutability in production. It also brings within its purview different kinds of labour, while subsuming subsistence wage as a limiting possibility. Similarly the marginal utility approach to value theory can claim to be a more general approach, for it covers cases of joint production on the one hand and rare commodities on the other.

Marginalist economics proposes what may be called a 'unified' value theory, comprising both commodity and factor markets. It reconciles value in exchange with value in use, and seeks to explain exchange values in terms of the degree of scarcity of resources. The concept of margin gives it a technique whereby the degree of scarcity could be defined in relation to the want system of individuals constituting a society; all exchange values are thus conceived as emanating from a single source, utility. However, its field of application is severely restricted, it does not extend beyond 'statics'. The assumption of perfect competition on which most of its theorems rest robs it further of its explanatory potency – market structures have increasingly moved away from the model of 'unlimited competition' since Cournot formulated it. The system does answer Jevons's questions; it does set out conditions of utility maximization under given constraints. But it does not answer the questions on accumulation and growth which classical political economy had posed; indeed it bypasses those questions.[33]

---

[33]Referring to the marginalist system of economics, G. L. S. Shackle observes: 'The 40 years from 1870 saw the creation of a Great Theory or Grand System of Economics, in one sense complete and self-sufficient, able on its own terms, to answer all questions which these terms allowed.' G. L. S. Shackle, *The Years of High Theory* (Cambridge University Press, Cambridge, 1967), p. 4; quoted in Maurice Dobb, *Theories of Value and Distribution since Adam Smith*, p. 167. Shackle may be right. But he seems to forget that any theory, worth

The New Liberalism

To have brought the various commodity markets and factor markets under one common principle of marginal valuation must be recognized as a scientific achievement. There is indeed a technical virtuosity in the marginalist system, which is appealing.[34] Much of the success of the system, despite its limitations, is undoubtedly due to this appeal.

One doubts, however, that this is all. Criticism of classical political economy along marginalist lines is much older than Jevons and Menger. Samuel Bailey's critique of the labour theory came just two years after the death of Ricardo.[35] And Robert Torrens, we are told, made special mention of Bailey's critique only seven years later, while arguing, at the Political Economy Club, that the theories of Ricardo had all proved erroneous.[36] While Bailey merely suggests 'choice and preference', in place of labour, as the source of exchange value, F. W. Lloyd gave a clear enunciation of a marginal utility theory of value as early as 1834. In the same year Mountifort Longfield gave a general theory of distribution which was clearly an anticipation of the marginal productivity theory.[37]

Surely there was no geographical obstacle to the circulation of these innovations; Lloyd spoke from Oxford, and Longfield spoke from Dublin. Yet they remained obscure. Classical political economy survived. When, in the now notorious passage in his *Principles*, John Stuart Mill claimed 'there is nothing in the laws of value which remains (1848) for the present or any future writer

---

the name, should be able to answer questions which its 'own terms' allowed. What, however, is important is to ask what these terms are and how relevant they are as a guide to the interpretation of phenomena in which one is interested.

[34]Jevons's enunciation of the economic problem, let us recall, is a clear invitation to a mathematical solution in terms of maxima and minima.

[35]See S. Bailey, *A Critical Dissertation on the Nature, Measures and Causes of Value* (1825) (LSE reprint, 1931).

[36]See J. L. Mallet's *Diaries* (Political Economy Club, vol. VI, London, 1921). Mallet notes in his *Diaries* (January 13, 1831): 'Torrens held that all the great principles of Ricardo's work had been successively abandoned, and that his theories of Value, Rent and Profits were now generally acknowledged to have been erroneous. As to Value the dissertation on the measure of value published in 1825 by Mr Baillie of Leeds has settled the question.'

[37]See F. W. Lloyd, *A Lecture of the Notion of Value* (1834), reprinted in *The Economic Journal*, May, 1927; also M. Longfield, *Lectures on Political Economy* (1934) (LSE reprint, 1931).

to clear up',[38] the 'laws' for which he was putting up his claim were clearly those that he inherited from Ricardo. Mill was essentially a Ricardian not only in his theory of distribution but also in his theory of value; if he uses the term 'cost of production' to define value, it is Ricardian 'labour and time' to which he alludes, not 'wages and profits'. Yet, within just two decades of Jevons's enunciation of the marginalist principle, marginalism became an established system of economic theory; indeed the last quarter of the nineteenth century saw a complete breakaway from classical political economy.

There is reason to believe that the marginalists' quest for an alternative approach to economic theory, ostensibly a scientific quest, had inherently a political purpose. The link between the advent of marginalism and the socialist movement of the time seems unmistakeable. Ricardo accepted capitalism and rationalized it in terms of its potential for progress.[39] He was a liberal, even as Smith was, and he believed in free trade and free enterprise. Yet, paradoxically, his theories of value and distribution contained elements that were soon to be employed towards its repudiation. Implicit in Ricardo's demonstration that wages are inversely related to profits, there is, as we have seen, a recognition of the inevitability of class conflict in a capitalist economy; and a theory of exploitation is a logical corollary of Ricardo's labour theory of value and his subsistence theory of wages. It was inevitable that these deductions were to be carried out sooner or later. An anti-capitalist critique indeed grew up, even during the so-called 'Ricardian period', based on the implications of classical political economy. Karl Marx's theory of class war is a logical development of this critique.[40] It seems clear that marginalism is a reaction to this. Marginalists not only repudiate the classical theories of value and distribution; they also repudiate the social and political implications of these theories. The marginalist system marks a revival of economic liberalism as against its socialist critique. Social relations are given an altogether new orientation in the new system. Class conflict is ruled out. So is

[38] J. S. Mill, *Principles*, book III, ch. 1, p. 436.
[39] It does not seem fair to allege, as Marx does, that Ricardo considered capitalism to be an 'absolute form' of productive organization. It was enough for him to have accepted it as the existing form and to build up theories on it.
[40] Marx writes a long chapter, giving an elaborate description of the works of some of his forerunners who opposed the capitalist system while building on Ricardian economics. See Karl Marx, *Theories of Surplus Value* (Foreign Languages Publishing House, Moscow, 1971), vol. III, ch. XXI.

exploitation. Jevons, for example, views the relations between labour and capital as one of co-operation. He quotes with approval from W. E. Hearn's *Plutology*, wherein labour and capital are shown as a kind of 'partnership' and as having a 'community of interest'. It is true that 'workmen are not their own capitalists' and that this fact introduces complexity into the problem'; the capitalists 'enter as a distinct interest'. Yet, he argues, competition resolves the possible conflict between the interest of the two parties; capital earns only the market rate of interest, while the workman ultimately receives the 'due value of his produce'. Jevons dismisses Ricardo's theory of the inverse relation between profits and wages as 'radically fallacious', thus cutting at the root of the theory of class war.[41] Later marginalists, J. B. Clark in particular, follow this up, arguing that labour and capital are both paid according to their marginal contribution to the total product, and that competition brings it about that the economy is left with zero surplus. 'Free competition', Clark argues, 'tends to give to labour what labour creates, to capitalists what capital creates, and to *entrepreneurs* what the coordinating function creates.'[42] Clark explicitly dismisses the socialist theory of exploitation. Thus he says: 'Property is protected at the point of its origin, if the actual wages are the whole product of labour, if interest is the product of capital, and if profit is the product of a coordinating act.'[43]

Marginalism came as a challenge to classical political economy. Yet it retains the basic social philosophy of Smith and Ricardo. The founders of marginalist economics were upholders of free trade and free enterprise. Thus Jevons argues against customs duties of any sort. 'Customs duties may be requisite as a means of raising revenue, but the time is passed when any economist should give the slightest countenance to their employment for interfering with the natural tendency of exchange to increase utility.'[44] Walras gave the principle a more rigorous form. His production equations are designed to show how, under free competition, *'services can be combined and converted into products of such a nature and in such quantities as will give the greatest*

---

[41]See on this, W. S. Jevons, *Theory*, pp. 267–75.
[42]J. B. Clark, *The Distribution of Wealth*, p. 3.
[43]Ibid., p. 9. Contrast this with Marx's theory of accumulation. Marx, as we have seen, attributes the origin of capital accumulation to 'force' and its continuance to the 'coercive power' of the capitalists over wage labour.
[44]W. S. Jevons, *Theory*, p. 246.

possible satisfaction of wants.'[45] Thus it is, Walras claims, that the case for free trade and free enterprise is proved.

There is, however, a difference, an important difference, between the old liberalism and the new. Classical social philosophy just does not go comfortably with classical political economy. Indeed it is a puzzle that the classical economists, Smith and Ricardo in particular, should have upheld the policy of free trade and free enterprise while their theory exhibited disharmony in social relations under the system. 'The problem', as Myrdal puts it, 'is not how did the socialists reach their revolutionary conclusions, but rather how did the classics reach their conservative conclusions.'[46]

The answer seems to be that to the classical economists the overriding consideration guiding policy was the creation of conditions which would stimulate accumulation. If Ricardo, for example, considered profit as the centre-piece of his theory of distribution, it is because he considered profit to be the source of accumulation, and hence of economic progress. It was the conviction of classical economists that freedom of enterprise was a necessary condition for sustained economic progress. If the liberalism of the marginalists is dictated by considerations of 'allocational efficiency', the liberalism of the classics was dictated by considerations of what may be called 'technological efficiency'.

[45]L. Walras, *Elements* (English translation, George Allen & Unwin, London, 1954), lesson 22, p. 255. Italics original. The famous Pareto optimum is a follow up of this Walrasian proposition. The position of maximum utility is defined by Pareto as being such that 'any small displacement in departing from that position necessarily has the effect of increasing the ophemility which certain individuals enjoy, and decreasing that which others enjoy'. (See V. Pareto, *Manual of Political Economy* (English translation, Macmillan, New York, 1971), ch. VI, sect. 33.

Notice that in this demonstration the distribution of property is taken as given. The 'maximum' which Walras derives from his equations is therefore a dubious maximum. See on this K. Wicksell, *Lectures on Political Economy*, ed. L. Robbins, (George Routledge & Sons, London, 1934), vol. I, pp. 74–9. Wicksell considers Walras's proposition to be wrong, in so far, especially, as it relates to an economy with unequal distribution of property. William Jaffe, translator of the *Elements*, however, defends Walras, saying that he eschewed considerations involving interpersonal comparison of utility, as did Pareto (L. Walras, *Elements*, Translator's Note to Lesson 10, pp. 510–11). The interpretation seems to be valid; Walras in his 'pure theory' did indeed propose to eschew considerations of 'human relations arising from the appropriation of social wealth' (ibid., p. 79). Earlier Jevons had also declared that his analysis of value was free of interpersonal comparison of utility (W. S. Jevons, *Theory*, p. 14). It should be noted, however, that eschewing considerations of property relations is one way of evading the issue of social conflict.

[46]Gunnar Myrdal, *Political Element in the Development of Economic Theory* (English translation, Paul Streeten, London, 1953), p. 108.

Now, these two criteria are substantially different. In the one the framework is static, where the intrinsic efficiency of a unit of each factor is assumed to be given. In the other the framework is dynamic where, in so far as innovations accompany accumulation, allowance is made for the possibility of an improvement in the intrinsic productive capacity of resources. Technological efficiency thus takes account of increasing returns or, as Adam Smith would put it, economies of division of labour. This of course is alien to marginalist economics.

Thus here again there is a pronounced discontinuity in economic thought. The classical economists accepted capitalism with full awareness of the disharmony in social relations which it tends to generate. Living at a time when the economy was absorbing the first impact of the industrial revolution they were inclined to show a special concern for growth, and to leave distributional anomalies alone. The marginalists, on the other hand, being already in the midst of labour discontent, recoiled from the theory which inspired it. Thus their chief concern was to show how socialism would result in a misallocation of resources. Some, like Jevons and Clark, dismissed the theory of social disharmony as false, except where competition is hampered; others, like Walras, left the problem of property distribution alone, as being outside the purview of their science.

7

A Neo-Classical Synthesis: Alfred Marshall

Salient Features

Alfred Marshall belonged to the marginalist epoch. He was indeed one of the independent discoverers of the marginal principle. Already in 1874, in his review of Jevons's *Theory* he made it clear that the marginal approach which Jevons adopted was not new to him. 'It is a familiar truth', Marshall claimed in course of the review, 'that the total utility of any commodity is not proportional to "its final degree of utility", i.e. the utility of that portion of it which we are only just induced to part with, or to put ourselves in the trouble of procuring, as the case may be.'[1] His own theory, however, received its final form in his *Principles of Economics*, published in 1890. In it he went vastly beyond Jevons. Not only did he translate what in Jevons was just a utility curve into a full-fledged theory of demand, he also integrated the latter into a theory of competitive equilibrium, comprising factor markets as well as commodity markets. Indeed, as we now know, thanks to the publication of his *Early Writings*, Marshall's formulation of the marginal productivity theory of factor prices is as old as Wicksteed's formulation. These early notes show that not only did he work out the theory in terms of partial derivatives of a production function, he also posed the adding-up problem asking, as Wicksteed did, if the sum of factor prices paid according to the marginal productivity rule comes out to be equal to the total product. 'The remuneration for the last dose of capital and labour equals $i\Delta c + w\Delta l$. But the whole produce is p and is that $ic + wl$?' His answer is, 'Yes because the higher parts

[1] *Memorials of Alfred Marshall*, ed. A. C. Pigou (Macmillan, London, 1925), p. 95.

fall in value'.[2] Although he abandoned this formal quest and later in the *Principles* qualified the doctrine of marginal productivity by the insertion of 'net' before 'product', apparently to take account of a possible element of joint demand, Marshall must be acknowledged as one of the pioneers of the new approach to the theory of distribution. The principle of substitution, which is the hallmark of marginalism, plays a crucial role in Marshall's theory of value and distribution. The universal principle of diminishing return, the striving on the part of entrepreneurs to minimize cost of production by carrying the employment of resources up to 'the margin of profitableness', the demonstration that it is this striving that results in the correspondence of prices of factors to their respective marginal productivities – these are among the salient features of Marshall's theory of value and distribution. In all this he comes close to Walras. Indeed Marshall, like Walras, works out a 'general equilibrium' system where account is taken of the interrelation of commodities and of factors of production. And although in his analysis of the market for commodities, he limits his inquiry to a single commodity, assuming that the market for it is independent of the prices of other commodities, his analysis of the market for factors of production does take account of possible interrelations; the famous 'partial equilibrium method' is applied to the commodity market, not to the market for factors of production.[3]

In his analysis of the implications of the marginal utility principle, however, Marshall goes beyond Walras, or indeed any of his contemporaries. Whereas Walras uses the concept of marginal utility as a 'ladder' (as Schumpeter would say) which he could later discard, for Marshall the approach has a significance of its own. Relating a marginal utility schedule to the demand schedule of a consumer, Marshall derives his well-known concept of consumer's surplus. The

---

[2]*The Early Economic Writings of Alfred Marshall, 1867–1890*, ed. J. K. Whitaker (Royal Economic Society, 1975), vol. 2, p. 323.

[3]See Alfred Marshall, *Principles of Economics* (Variorum, vol. 1, Macmillan, 1961), Mathematical Appendix XXI, where the problem of interrelations (joint demand and joint supply on the one hand and joint supply and composite supply on the other) is solved by simultaneous equations, showing that the number of equations just e ;uals the number of unknowns. The solution, let it be noted, is an answer to the problem of iₑentifying the marginal product of a factor where technology imposes limits to the variability of its proportion in a process of production. If, in his famous example of 'a marginal employee' (ibid., pp. 515–16), the marginal shepherd needed a crook, the supply price of the crook would have to be deduced from the general equilibrium system and deducted from the gross marginal product of the shepherd before the wages of shepherds could be determined. Hence the insertion 'net'. Hence also Marshall's reluctance to accept the marginal productivity theory as a complete theory of distribution.

construction is designed to exhibit how, contrary to the belief of the so-called 'harmony' economists, the market equilibrium which a free play of competitive forces is supposed to lead up to is not necessarily a position of maximum social welfare. Marshall's demand analysis thus takes him beyond the market over to what later came to be known as welfare economics.

This, however, is only a part of the story. Marshall no doubt uses the marginal technique in his theory of value and distribution, relating commodity prices to marginal utility and factor prices to marginal productivity, but he does not go far with his marginalist contemporaries. It is not true, he insists, that the theory of demand is the scientific basis of economics.[4] The problem of economics, as he views it, is not just a problem of the allocation of *given* resources; for him the problem involves a study of how the resources come to be what they are. Even where he invokes a stationary state as an analytical device, stationariness, as he contemplates it, is not just a hypothesis, as the marginalists would take it to be, but is itself the resultant of a balancing of forces which tend to change; Marshall's economics is not confined just to the analysis of an equilibrium situation, it extends to an analysis of the process by which equilibrium is established.

Now this is an approach which has a special significance for Marshall's analytical system. Methodologically, Marshall's analysis of equilibrium points to a dynamic element, even though it bears a static garb. The equilibrium that is envisaged is worked out within the framework of a stationary state, so that the end point exhibits relationships which have a static character. Yet the analysis of the process which is supposed to lead to equilibrium is dynamic in our sense of the term; the process involves time and is thus irreversible. The dynamic element is indeed embedded in Marshall's statics – 'My Statics is indissolubly one with my Dynamics', he writes to J. B. Clark, questioning the usefulness of the latter's static method. We shall go into this in greater detail in the following section, where we discuss the character of Marshall's dynamics. There is, however, one matter which requires to be mentioned even at this stage. The method that Marshall adopts leads him inevitably to an analysis of the condition of supply; in the process towards equilibrium

[4]Ibid., book III, ch. II, p. 90. Not only does Marshall recognize what he calls a 'science of activity' as a necessary supplement to the 'science of wants', he goes further to suggest that 'if either, more than the other, may claim to be the interpreter of the history of man whether on the economic side or any other, it is the science of activities and not that of wants.'

Marshall allows variation in the supply, not only of commodities but also of factors, in so far as they are reproducible.

Now, this is a significant shift. It is a shift which brings into relief Marshall's affinity to Ricardian economics. Since the method allows time for resources to react to demand, it throws up a vital distinction between land and capital. In Marshall's 'dynamical' world, capital varies and has thus a schedule of supply prices, while land being fixed and invariable has no supply price. The distinction, Marshall urges, is important, for it brings out an essential truth in Ricardo's theory of diminishing returns and rent. Marshall recognizes the universal principle of diminishing returns. He also recognizes the fact that land is but one form of capital from an individual point of view, admitting that, in so far as land is transferable as between different crops, it does have a supply price from the point of view of a single crop. Yet, considering the social purpose of economic theory, he puts land on a special footing. Thus it is that diminishing return from a more intensive cultivation of land is seen by him as 'distinct from', though 'akin to', diminishing return from a disproportionate use of any individual factor of production. Thus also it is that rent of land is seen as the '*leading* species of a large genus'.[5]

Marshall upholds the Ricardian doctrine of rent as a price-determined surplus, even though he is acutely conscious of the caution with which it has to be understood and applied. 'It is *wisest not* to say', he writes to Edgeworth, 'that ''Rent does not enter into cost of production'': for that would confuse many people. But it is *wicked* to say that ''Rent *does* enter into cost of production'', because that is *sure* to be applied in such a way as to lead to the denial of subtle truths.'[6] Recognition of rent as a surplus is to Marshall, as it is to Ricardo, important not only from the point of view of public policy but also from the analytical point of view. 'If from the first', Marshall argues, as Ricardo would also, 'the state had retained true rents in its own hands, the vigour of industry and accumulation need not have been impaired.'[7] Further – and this is important from an analytical point of view – Marshall is interested, like Ricardo, or indeed Smith, in the enquiry as to whether, to use his own words, 'the cost of attaining a given result is increasing

---

[5]See,A. Marshall, *Principles*, book V, ch. VIII, sect. 4, pp. 407–9; also p. 412.
[6]See *Memorials of Alfred Marshall*, p. 436. Italics original.
[7]A. Marshall, *Principles*, p. 803.

or diminishing with changing economic conditions'.[8] In this enquiry the relevant concept is one of 'real cost', not 'expenses' as they are estimated by an individual entrepreneur. However, whereas Ricardo is content with labour alone for his rough measure of costs, Marshall's real costs consist of labour and 'waiting'; Marshall, like Mill, adopts Ricardo's amended labour theory of value.[9]

Where, then, does Alfred Marshall stand? Marshall's economics starts with the behaviour of an individual consumer or an individual firm, as does the economics of Jevons, Menger or Walras. Like them he relates commodity prices to marginal utility, and factor prices to marginal productivity. Substitution at the margin is a pervasive principle in his analytical system. He also, like his marginalist contemporaries, fixes his eyes in the ultimate analysis on the equilibrium of the market; the price–quantity relation subsisting at the point of equilibrium indeed plays an important part in the Marshallian system. Thus far Marshall's affinity to marginalist economics is clear. Yet when it comes to the analysis of the process through which equilibrium is established, his method differs very conspicuously from the method of Jevons or Walras; for here he finds himself drawn to an analysis of the condition of supply. In Marshall's system activities play at least as important a part as wants, and activities are the source of supply, as wants are the source of demand. So it is that Marshall, in spite of his allegiance to the marginalist principle, traces his ancestry to Ricardo. Referring to his *Principles* in a letter to N. G. Pierson, he writes: 'the book was written to express one idea; & one idea only. That idea is that whereas Ricardo & Co. maintain that value is determined by cost of production, & Jevons & (in a measure) the Austrians that it is determined by utility, each was right in what he affirmed but wrong

---

[8]Ibid., p. 350.

[9]In order to make the two elements of costs commensurate Marshall uses the measuring rod of money, assuming that the purchasing power of money in terms of labour and waiting remains constant. He, however, warns us that the correspondence of money costs to real costs 'is never to be assumed lightly'. Remember that this is just the old quest for an invariable standard which baffled Ricardo. Remember also that Ricardo discarded gold (or money) as a measure for just the reason for which Marshall prescribes caution in using it. While, however, Ricardo, as we have seen, eliminates time on the ground that its role is minor, Marshall does not. However, the point especially to note is that both eliminate land. Schumpeter regards Marshall's doctrine of real cost as 'the olive branch presented to his classical predecessors' (J. Schumpeter, *History of Economic Analysis* (George Allen & Unwin, London, 1954), p. 1057). If the interpretation here given is correct, then Schumpeter's remark would seem to be somewhat casual; surely the doctrine is more than a mere gesture to the classics.

in what he denied'.[10] Marshall's chief endeavour in value analysis is to indicate a junction between equilibrium economics and the economics of growth as a sequence in time. While accepting the marginal principle as a basis for the analysis of the behaviour of an individual consumer or an individual firm, and while, as a preliminary exercise, adhering to the framework of a stationary state, Marshall is anxious to show how the capitalist system operates on its way towards the assumed equilibrium state. Alfred Marshall is thus truly a 'neo-classic', whose approach points to a possible synthesis between the two strands of economic theory – the classical and the marginalist.[11]

How does he do it, and to what extent does he succeed?

Time Element

It is common knowledge that Marshall introduced the element of time in order to show the relative position of demand and supply as determinants of value. In the very short period – a 'day' – where the 'stock' of a commodity in the market is fixed, it is demand which plays the dominant role in the determination of value; one blade of the pair of scissors being held still, the other blade is supposed to do the cutting. When, however, commodities appear as a 'flow' over time, supply comes to its own, for it is then flexible.[12] Given time, the supply of a commodity reacts to price, in so far as it is

---

[10]*Early Economic Writings*, vol. 1, pp. 97–8.

[11]It needs to be emphasized that it is a creative exercise, and not merely an attempt at a compromise with Ricardo, as critics often seem to think. Marshall would resent an interpretation which suggests that his introduction of a supply function was only a gesture to the classics. Observe what he writes to J. B. Clark: 'One thing alone in American Criticism irritates me, though it be not unkindly meant. It is the suggestion that I try to "compromise between" or "reconcile" divergent schools of thought. Such work seems to me trumpery. Truth is the only thing worth having: not peace' (*Memorials of Alfred Marshall*, p. 418).

[12]Marshall was very particular about this stock-flow distinction in the context of his time analysis. In a paper on distribution and exchange he writes: 'The fact is, that twenty years ago I abandoned the use of curves for market problems because they were not really wanted; and I found people would not heed the note of warning that the curves for the normal problem relate to *rates* of production and consumption and those for market curves [sic] to amounts bought and sold' ('Distribution and Exchange', *Economic Journal*, vol. VIII, p. 46). He makes the same point in one of his letters to Edgeworth: 'You know I never apply curves or mathematics for market values . . . I found that if I got people to use Demand and Supply curves which discussed *Stocks* along the axis of *x*, they could not easily be kept from introducing the notion of stock when *flow* was essential' (*Memorials of Alfred Marshall*, p. 435).

reproducible, even as demand reacts to price. One thus needs the supply function as well as the demand function in one's search for the equilibrium price of a commodity.

This, however, is not all. Marshall's time analysis involves more than a mere reminder that when there are two unknowns – price and output – we need two equations for a solution of the problem of determinateness of equilibrium. The exercise involves an attempt at a rehabilitation of the classical problem of progress of an economy over time.

Let us see how the method works. Let us begin by considering what Marshall calls 'market value' – the price of a commodity on a 'day', assuming that the stock available in the market is fixed. We borrow Marshall's famous example of a corn market in a country town. The sellers are supposed to hold corn and the buyers are supposed to hold money. Marshall's own table showing the demand and supply of corn is reproduced below:

At the price	Holders will be willing to sell	Buyers will be willing to buy
37s per quarter	1000 quarters	600 quarters
36s per quarter	700 quarters	700 quarters
35s per quarter	600 quarters	900 quarters

Clearly, as the table shows, the equilibrium price is 36s per quarter, for at that price both the buyers and the sellers would agree to an exchange of 700 quarters of corn, the marginal utility of corn in terms of money being at that level the same for both parties.

How is the equilibrium arrived at? In the beginning there is darkness. Each is ignorant of the relative marginal utility scales of the other. Nor are the parties supposed to acquire knowledge of each other's bargaining position through a process of 'crying of prices' or of 'recontracting'. Unlike Walras and Edgeworth, Marshall allows actual transactions to take place at prices other than the equilibrium price. There is in his exercise a beginning rate and a final rate; the market may begin at 37s per quarter, or it may begin at 35s per quarter, depending upon the relative bargaining strength of the two parties. Where, then, will the market settle down? Note that it makes a difference whether the early transactions take place at rates nearer to 37s or to 35s; for any given amount of corn exchanged, the amount of money passing from the buyer to the seller will be larger if transactions begin from the upper end than it would be if they were to begin from the lower end. Note also that once a transaction is made, it is *irreversible*. How far, then, could one depend on the process to lead up to a determinate equilibrium, such as one would read off from the table? Marshall neglects the income effects due to transfer of money, arguing that in a single market the amount of money transferred in the process of buying and selling forms such a small part of the total resources of the people that the marginal utility of money may for all practical purposes be assumed to remain constant. The marginal utility of the 700th quarter of corn is 36s to both buyers and sellers, whatever may have been the prices at which the earlier transactions were made.

Thus, on the day which we take as our base, the market starts with a stock of, say, 1000 quarters of corn. Of this 700 quarters are sold, and 300 quarters are retained for the sellers' own consumption. The market is cleared at a final rate, 36s per quarter of corn. The amount of money that passes from the buyers to the sellers is, however, still indeterminate, for it depends upon the initial prices and the intermediate prices at which the earlier transactions take place. Now, suppose – and this follows from Marshall's assumption of constant marginal utility of money – that the demand and supply schedules remain unaltered and the market opens with the same stock of corn on the following day. The market would then in all probability start straight at 36s per quarter, for there is now one new element in the situation – the buyers and sellers have knowledge of the equilibrium price. Marshall could thus visualize a 'true equilibrium', where, learning from experience, buyers and sellers 'hit upon' the equilibrium rate of exchange and 'adhere to it throughout'. And when this happens, not only the amount of corn bought but also the amount of money exchanged becomes determinate.

Marshall's partial equilibrium is thus determinate, even though transactions are allowed to take place at 'false prices' (as Hicks calls them), since one of the things that are exchanged is the general medium of exchange, whose marginal utility is assumed to remain constant.

However, while buyers may be supposed to spend a small part of their income on any single commodity so that their income effect may be neglected, it is not clear how sellers would be affected. For sellers, whose earnings depend upon the price of their commodity in the market, the income effect of changes in price may be significant. Marshall cites the instance of the labour market. To the seller of labour whose income depends solely upon the rate at which wages are settled in the market, it matters greatly whether the initial rates are high or low; the marginal utility of money to him does not remain constant, and if he begins with a disadvantage he ends up also with a disadvantage.[13] The process, Marshall tells us, tends to be cumulative. In so far as the labourer starts with a wage rate which is lower than the equilibrium rate, his efficiency as a worker is lowered. This lowers the equilibrium rate itself, while the lowering of the equilibrium rate in its turn further reduces his bargaining strength.[14] This, Marshall urges, distinguishes the labour market from any other market. For markets for commodities the advantage in bargaining, he thinks, is likely to be 'pretty well distributed between the two sides'.

Let us then revert to the corn-market case which, on Marshall's assumption, admits of a determinate equilibrium. Let us remind ourselves that the determinateness of equilibrium is shown to be the resultant of a process which is marked by transactions at 'false' prices, which are irreversible. Already therefore Marshall introduces a method which, in our sense, is dynamic, even though the process is supposed to lead on to a 'true' equilibrium state, the same stock of corn being cleared each day at the same price.

It is the same method that Marshall pursues when he extends his perspective to cover production.[15] On a day, Marshall's day, the stock of the commodity is fixed, so the cost incurred in producing it and in bringing it to the market is irrelevant – 'bygones are for ever bygones', as Jevons declared. But when time is allowed for production to take place, supply becomes flexible and it reacts to

[13]On how, when the assumption of constant marginal utility of money is dropped, the equilibrium becomes indeterminate, see Marshall, *Principles*, Appendix F on Barter. Hicks suggests an alternative assumption to support determinateness of equilibrium. For equilibrium to be determinate it is not necessary, he argues, that the marginal utility of money to the traders should be constant. All that is necessary is that the income effects of buyers and sellers, which run in opposite directions, should cancel out (J. R. Hicks, *Value and Capital* (Oxford University Press, Oxford, 1939), p. 129). This is true in so far as the problem is one of market clearings only. But it breaks down when the problem is one of the relative position of the buyers and the sellers, as it turns out to be as a result of trading at 'false' prices.
[14]See A. Marshall, *Principles*, p. 569. This is the kind of cumulative process which Gunnar Myrdal seems to have extended to the analysis of the position of underdeveloped economies in their trade with the developed economies (see G. Myrdal, *Economic Theory and Underdeveloped Regions* (Vora & Co., Bombay, 1958), especially ch. 2).
[15]This is precisely why we have allowed ourselves to take such elaborate notice of operations in the ultra-short period market.

price. Marshall's division of time into a short period and a long period is designed to bring out the nature of this reaction. In the short period, while the supply of the commodity is not fixed, it is not fully flexible either; some resources, like machinery or specialized skill, are fixed, and hence production is constrained. In the corn-market case, for example, while the supply of seeds may be flexible, the supply of tractors is not. Production of corn thus encounters resistance from tractors, much in the same way as it encounters resistance from land in the Ricardian system; fixed capital behaves like land in the short period, and its return behaves like rent; Marshall calls it quasi-rent. Further, since in reality there are different kinds of fixed capital, some having a longer service tenure than others, or requiring longer time for construction, production encounters different degrees of resistance as time is extended; there are thus several short periods that intervene as the industry moves towards the long period equilibrium. In the long period, as Marshall defines it, there is full flexibility – 'all investments of capital and effort in providing the material plant and organization of business, and in acquiring trade knowledge and specialized ability, have time to be adjusted to the incomes which are expected to be earned by them'.[16]

Long period normal price of a commodity (here corn) is one which, if hit upon at the very beginning and adhered to throughout, would keep the industry in equilibrium condition all along; the *rate* of production and consumption would thus remain constant through time, with the price of the product equal to its cost of production. This means, now that we are taking account of production, not only that the output of the commodity remains constant but also that the resources needed for its production (here tractors and seeds) are maintained in an appropriate relation with the output. This involves perfect foresight. 'A theoretically perfect long period', Marshall reminds us, 'must give time enough to enable not only the factors of production of the commodity to be adjusted to demand, but also the factors of production of those factors of production and so on; and this, when carried to its logical consequences, will be found to involve the supposition of a stationary state of industry.'[17]

[16]For the definition of short period and long period, see A. Marshall, *Principles*, pp. 376–7.
[17]Ibid., p. 379n.

Marshall's long period equilibrium is clearly a static equilibrium. The demand curve that it postulates is a static curve; the speed of reaction of demand to price is assumed to be so high that time is just eliminated. Production however is a technical process; it does not respond so readily to price variations. Yet in the perspective of the long period, the supply curve is shown to behave as a static curve. Full flexibility is assumed in the supply, so that in the equilibrium condition the price of the commodity conforms to its cost of production, and we have a stationary state.[18] Is not, then, one will ask, the long period equilibrium of Marshall a kind of equilibrium with which Walras had already in a more general setting made us familiar? For, in the Walrasian system, too, there is implicit in the equilibrium condition an equation between costs and prices; factor price equilibrium cannot surely be consistent with commodity price equilibrium unless prices of commodities are equal to their costs of production.

This, however, is not all that Marshall's method stands for. If it did, then all the exercises that we are taken through in the context of the corn market in a country town – transactions at 'false' prices, the irreversibility hypothesis etc. – would appear to be an unnecessary detour. It is here suggested that the distinctive character of Marshall's method is the analysis of a process, a sustained process, which derives stimulus from the activities of the organizer of industry ('industrial undertaker' as Marshall would like to call him). It is an irreversible, hence a dynamic, process which marks the progress of the industry. Thus the short period plays a crucial role in Marshall's time analysis. The typical Marshallian concepts, quasi-rent, supplementary cost and prime cost, belong to the short period. Short period prices are our familiar 'false' prices when considered in relation to the long period equilibrium. The costs that are relevant to short period prices are prime costs.[19] These costs vary with

---

[18]In so far as Marshall's analysis concentrates on a single industry, cost is supposed to be 'money cost'; an individual industry takes factor prices from the general factor market. However, as we noted earlier, the money cost is assumed by Marshall to be a reflection of 'real cost'. There is therefore no circular reasoning here.

[19]Marshall includes in prime costs not only wages of that part of labour which is paid by the hour or by the piece, but also the 'raw material used' and the 'extra wear-and-tear of the plant' (A. Marshall, *Principles*, p. 360). In the face of this clear enunciation, it is difficult to know why Hicks should have thought that Marshall's short period analysis 'left out what Keynes was later to call user cost' (J. R. Hicks, *Capital and Growth* (Oxford University Press, Oxford, 1965), p. 52). For, are not raw materials used and wear-and-tear of machinery what constitute Keynes's 'user cost'?

output, and thus set the limit below which the short period price is not allowed to fall; usually, though, it covers a part of the supplementary cost also. If there is overinvestment in fixed capital in the industry, the short period price covers less than the proper share of the supplementary cost – in other words, quasi-rent falls below the normal rate of interest. When, on the other hand, there is underinvestment and a consequent deficiency in fixed capital, the short period price covers more than the proper share of the supplementary cost and quasi-rent rises above the normal rate of interest.[20] The technique of production, however, remains constant, for factor prices are given from outside and are supposed to remain constant. It is via these short period 'false' transactions that producers acquire knowledge and move on towards the final long period equilibrium state.

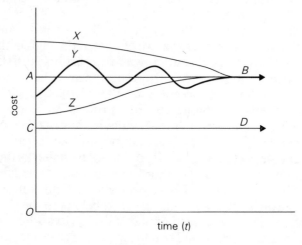

FIGURE 4

The progress of prices through time can be exhibited as in figure 4. Measure time t along the horizontal axis. Let OA be the aggregate cost per unit of the commodity, of which OC is the prime cost and CA is the supplementary cost. The long period equilibrium price is OA. The industry would be in a stationary state along AB if price OA were hit upon at the very beginning and adhered to throughout. As it is, in the

[20]'The supplementary costs, which the owner of a factory expects to be able to add to prime costs, are the source of the quasi-rent which it will yield to him' (A. Marshall, *Principles*, p. 362n). For a definition of prime costs and supplementary costs, see ibid., pp. 356–60.

absence of perfect foresight, short period prices would deviate from the long period equilibrium price. Three possibilities are shown – all leading ultimately to the stationary state. Curves X and Z show smooth progress towards the stationary state; the former starts from an upper level where the short period price covers more than the proper share of the supplementary cost and where the quasi-rent is higher than the normal rate of interest, while the latter starts from a lower level where the short period price covers less than the proper share of the supplementary cost and where the quasi-rent is lower than the normal rate of interest. Curve Y shows vicissitudes – sometimes rising above AB and sometimes falling below it, yet ultimately coalescing with AB.[21]

This certainly is in the Ricardian tradition. Curve X looks very Ricardian indeed. The analogy should not, however, be pushed far. In Ricardo's analysis, which comprises the entire economy – at any rate, as it gets out of the corn model – demand is embedded in supply; in the context of the aggregate economy supply is supposed to create demand. The obstacle to an indefinite growth arises from the scarcity of land. In Marshall's analysis, which is confined to a single industry, land is not scarce, except in so far as it is specific to the industry; if therefore the long period equilibrium is associated with a stationary state, the situation has apparently to be explained in terms of the constancy of the demand curve. Marshall assumes conditions outside the industry to remain constant, as the industry proceeds towards equilibrium. His famous 'pound of *caeteris paribus*' not only ensures that the technique of production in the industry remains constant, it also ensures that the demand curve, which is (largely at any rate) given from outside, remains constant.[22]

The outline of the model gets blurred, however, once conditions outside the industry are allowed to change; and the longer the period that is required for the tendency to full equilibrium to work itself out,

---

[21]The short period prices, as shown in figure 4, are not allowed in any of these cases to touch the prime cost line CD. This is in accordance with Marshall's hypothesis that firms, 'for fear of spoiling the market', see to it that the price in any case covers not only the whole of the prime cost but also a share of the supplementary cost.

[22]The interpretation of Marshall's period analysis suggested here is somewhat different, formally at any rate, from Hicks's interpretation (J. R. Hicks, *Capital and Growth*, pp. 49–52). Hicks describes Marshall's method as static, as he considers Ricardo's analysis to be also static. Marshall's periods, Hicks argues, are 'self-contained', as Ricardo's periods also are, and hence static. We, on the other hand, apply the irreversibility criterion and consider both as belonging to a dynamic process, one period leading on to another.

the greater is the possibility that conditions would change. This apart, as the industry grows in its progress towards long-term equilibrium, it may – and often does – develop economies due to division of labour and specialization. If this happens, the supply price falls as output increases; the industry then is subject to what Marshall calls increasing returns. In short periods, where supply is constrained by a fixed stock of capital, material and human, diminishing return is the rule. Not so, Marshall argues, in the long period. When enough time is allowed for plants to be adapted to the condition of demand and for specialized skill to develop, the efficiency of factors tends to increase and consequently the cost per unit of the product tends to decrease; the long period supply curve may thus be downward sloping.

Now, under such conditions the marginal technique breaks down – costs relate to the 'whole process of production', not to a 'parcel of product'. So does the static method; the supply curve under conditions of increasing returns represents points which are irreversible, being associated with different levels of economies of production.[23] Here clearly Marshall moves away from marginalist economics and comes closer to the classics. He yet retains the concept of equilibrium. In spite of falling supply prices, he argues there is a limit to the growth of the industry; there is equilibrium at a point where the supply price tends to fall at a steeper rate than the rate at which the demand price falls.[24] Marshall's theory of increasing returns thus takes on a Smithian character; division of labour is shown to be limited by the extent of the market.

All this exercise, let us remember, is restricted to an analysis of the progress of a single industry, as it occurs through time as a result of the endeavour on the part of organizers of business to adjust

[23]For all this, see A. Marshall, *Principles*, Appendix H. Schumpeter objects to the procedure that Marshall adopts in the context of increasing returns. 'Marshall', he complains, 'insisted on including internal and external economies in his (industrial) supply schedules . . . in spite of the fact that he thereby destroyed their reversibility and rendered them useless for purposes of static theory' (J. Schumpeter, *History of Economic Analysis*, p. 1046). So what? – Marshall would perhaps retort. In the perspective that he holds here, it is static theory that he would reject; he would surely ask us to adjust theory to facts rather than facts to theory! One would indeed be inclined to suggest that the debate as to whether increasing return is compatible with competitive equilibrium – a debate which Schumpeter apparently has in mind – is in this overtly dynamic context somewhat misplaced. Once you move away from statics, perfect competition ceases to have the attribute which Cournot or Walras gives it; it takes on the character, Marshall believes, of a struggle for survival.

[24]Marshall recognizes the possibility of multiple positions of equilibrium in such cases. Yet since it is a case of the product of a single industry, for which, while the supply price remains always positive, the demand has a satiety level, there must be at least one position of stable equilibrium.

the supply of the product, and of the resources that go into the process of production, to the condition of demand. The partial equilibrium method enables Marshall to isolate the happenings in a single industry from those of the rest of the economy. Clearly the method is not intended for the analysis of the growth of the economy as a whole; accumulation is not covered by the method.[25]

Doctrine of Maximum Satisfaction

One of the simplifications that Marshall did in the context of his partial equilibrium analysis is, as we have seen, to assume that the marginal utility of money remains constant in the course of the progress of the industry. The assumption is double edged in its operation in Marshall's system. While, as we saw, it ensures determinateness of equilibrium, it also provides a yardstick for measuring the utility of a commodity. Marshall measures consumer's surplus, using money as the yardstick.[26] The excess of the price which a consumer 'would be willing to pay' over the price which he 'actually does pay' for a commodity is the money measure of a surplus of utility which he enjoys from the purchase of the commodity. The measure is unambiguous, Marshall argues, when the marginal utility of money that is given up in exchange remains invariant to the amount purchased.

Marshall's concept of consumers' surplus is designed with a view to an analysis of the implications of the long period equilibrium state, which he worked out in terms of an equation between prices

[25]There is evidence that Marshall intended to work out a macro-economic model of growth equilibrium on the basis of a production function, anticipating what is today called the 'neo-classical growth model' (see *Early Economic Writings*, vol. 2, pp. 305–16). If he did not pursue the exercise, it is presumably because he saw that it was not possible to reconcile the production function approach with a theory of growth equilibrium, where the conditions of production, exchange and distribution are supposed to maintain constant relations with one another. In the *Principles* he does not go beyond enunciating the conditions of growth equilibrium (see p. 368).

[26]The concept relates primarily to an individual; hence the apostrophe *before* 's'. It is later extended to cover groups of individuals also. When it is a question of a comparison of the surplus of one group with that of another, Marshall assumes that personal peculiarities of individuals forming these groups cancel out. In using the term in what follows, therefore, we shall put the apostrophe *after* 's'.

We are leaving out the variants of the concept of consumers' surplus, as brought out by Hicks (J. R. Hicks, 'Four Consumers' Surpluses', *Review of Economic Studies*, vol. xi, 1943). For when the marginal utility of money is held constant, they are all supposed to come to the same thing.

and costs. The question raised is whether the position of competitive equilibrium is in any sense one of maximum satisfaction. This, as we know, is the central question in the value analysis of Jevons and Walras. Whereas, however, Jevons and Walras were content with what happens to exchange relations at the position of competitive equilibrium, Marshall had misgivings.

Marshall judges welfare in terms of the net satisfaction which buyers and sellers derive from exchange. In a limited sense, he agrees, a position of equilibrium of demand and supply may be regarded as a position of maximum satisfaction. For, so long as the demand price is above the supply price, it is possible to imagine a price which would give a surplus of satisfaction to the buyer or to the seller, or to both. The marginal utility of what he receives is greater than what he gives up, to at least one of the two parties, while the other, if he does not gain by the exchange, yet does not lose by it.[27] This, let us remember, is just the proposition which was later to be elaborated by Pareto in the context of general equilibrium and which has since acquired the distinction of being called 'Pareto optimum' after the name of the author. Marshall, however, is not content with this limited interpretation. He argues that a movement away from the position of competitive equilibrium may often increase the aggregate satisfaction of the buyers and sellers taken together.

First, anticipating the major criticism of the concept of Pareto optimum, Marshall suggests that there are distributional anomalies in the society which distort exchange relations, so that a shift away from the position of competitive equilibrium may often confer a gain to one party which exceeds the loss to the other in terms of welfare. When, for example, the producers as a class are poorer than the consumers, the aggregate satisfaction from exchange might be increased, in so far as the demand is inelastic, by a stinting of supply.[28] The opposite happens when the consumers as a class are poorer than the producers. All this is, Marshall adds, 'a special case of the broad proposition that the aggregate satisfaction can prima facie be increased by the distribution, whether voluntarily or compulsorily, of some of the property of the rich among the poor'.[29] It seems clear that Marshall considers an

[27]A. Marshall, *Principles*, p. 470.
[28]Marshall here cites the possible case of a poor population of pearl divers dependent for food on a rich population who took pearls in exchange; ibid., p. 471*n*.
[29]Ibid., pp. 471–2.

equitable distribution of property to be a condition necessary for the validity of the doctrine of maximum satisfaction.

What, however, has figured more in Marshallian literature is the limitation of the doctrine which arises from the operation of increasing returns. In marginalist economics increasing return is an anachronism; static competitive equilibrium precludes its operation. In Marshall's 'dynamic' structure where firms 'grow and decay' on the way to equilibrium, the conditions of supply with respect to individual firms are not necessarily typical of the conditions of supply with respect to the industry – hence his recourse to the well-known device of the representative firm. The procedure admits increasing return for the representative firm, as for the industry, while both are in equilibrium. Hence the problem.

It is of the nature of (stable) equilibrium that for an output beyond the position of equilibrium the demand price is lower than the supply price. For industries subject to increasing returns, therefore, output is in equilibrium at a point where there is still scope for economies of production; demand happens here to be an obstacle to the society having the full benefit of economies of scale. When this happens, it is possible, Marshall argues, to devise terms of exchange which would be 'amply remunerative to producers, at the same time that they left a large balance of advantage to the consumers'. Thus if the producers could be induced to lower their supply schedule, so that the equilibrium position is shifted forward, the consumers might reap a benefit which is larger than the loss to the producers; they would indeed, if increasing returns operated sharply. 'One simple plan', Marshall suggests, 'would be the levying of a tax by the community on their own incomes . . . and devoting the tax to a bounty on the production of those goods with regard to which the law of increasing returns acts sharply.'[30] It is shown that in such cases the loss due to the bounty would be outweighed by the gain in consumers' surplus. Marshall demonstrates the proposition on a diagram as shown in figure 5.

In the figure, output is measured along Ox and price along Oy. DD' represents the demand curve of the industry, and SS' the supply curve, both sloping downward. The equilibrium is at A, where DD' intersects SS'. Let the new supply curve be ss', and the new equilibrium be at a, the bounty per unit of the commodity

[30]Ibid., p. 472. The proposition looks pretty much like what is today known as the compensation principle.

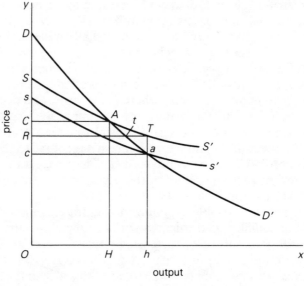

output

FIGURE 5

being *Ta. AH*, then, is the old equilibrium price and *ah* the equilibrium price after the bounty. Draw *AC* and *ac* parallel to *Ox* and let them meet *Oy* at *C* and *c* respectively. The increase of consumers' surplus is represented by *CcaA*, while the aggregate bounty is represented by *Rcat*. Thus the increase of consumers' surplus outweighs the bounty if *RCAt* is greater than *Tta*. It does indeed in the figure, where increasing returns are shown to operate sharply.[31]

A variant of the situation is where there is possibility of multiple positions of equilibrium. Under increasing return conditions the industry may have more than one position of (stable) equilibrium. In such cases it is clear that a movement from a lower equilibrium

[31]A. Marshall, *Principles*, p. 469n. The corresponding case of a tax on diminishing return industries is not considered here because, as Marshall warns us, there is an asymmetry between increasing returns and diminishing returns (as he defines them), the latter being due to a disproportionate use of factors of production and not due to what one might call diseconomies of production (diminishing return *from the standpoint of the community*, as distinct from diminishing return *simpliciter*, to use Pigou's felicitous terms). So, while it is true that a tax on a diminishing return industry results in a gain in terms of tax revenue which might outweigh the loss of consumers' surplus, the gain is swamped by the loss of landlords' rent due to a curtailment of output; the loss of consumers' surplus combined with the loss of rent can be shown necessarily to exceed the gain in tax revenue.

output to a higher equilibrium output increases consumers' surplus without the producers incurring any loss. Left to itself the industry would, in all probability, get stuck at the lower equilibrium point. If, however, by an appropriate bounty, the output is brought over to a higher equilibrium level, the aggregate satisfaction necessarily increases, for the bounty can be withdrawn as soon as the industry settles down at the new equilibrium level.

Marshall thus concludes that exchange relations are not always harmonious, that the free play of demand and supply does not necessarily lead to maximum aggregate satisfaction.[32]

For our purpose the significant point is that in all this exercise 'net utility' of consumers comes to the forefront as the entity to be maximized. Marshall here is a 'marginal utility' theorist, anxious to probe the implications of competitive equilibrium on the lines of Jevons and Walras; the answer that he proposes is different, but the question asked is the same as that which Jevons or Walras asked. If in his time analysis he inclines so heavily towards the classics, in his analysis of the implications of equilibrium he is truly a marginalist. The classical economists were in search of an index of prosperity and found it in the surplus of product over costs – both measured in labour. Marshall, on the other hand, is in search of an index of welfare, and he finds it in a surplus of satisfaction (or utility) over costs – both measured in money.

Marshall's Social Philosophy

Marshall, we know, had misgivings about the social implications of the capitalist system. He was not a believer in the beneficence of a competitive order; the position of competitive equilibrium, he argued, is not necessarily one of maximum social welfare, considered not only from the point of view of distribution but also from the point of view of the allocation of resources. He recognized the possibilities of unequal exchange leading to a cumulative deterioration of the party which begins with a low bargaining power. He was intensely aware of the conflict in this respect between the labouring class and the capitalist class. 'When a workman is in fear

[32]It should be of interest to note that both Marshall and Walras take Bastiat's *Economic Harmonies* as the point of reference in their analysis of the problem. Yet while Walras introduces it to 'prove' the proposition, Marshall introduces it to show its error.

of hunger, his need for money (its marginal utility to him) is very great, and he may go on selling his labour at a low rate.'[33] The peculiarities of the labour market, especially the poverty of the labouring class and the cumulative character of their disadvantage in bargaining, are indeed among the more conspicuous features of Marshall's theory of distribution.[34]

Yet, while he would urge ameliorative action on the part of the state in areas which are especially depressed, Marshall was against any attempt at a drastic reorganization of the society. As far back as 1885, in a paper to the Industrial Remuneration Conference, he declared: 'In a sense indeed I am a socialist, for I believe that almost every existing institution must be changed . . . But I fear socialists would refuse to admit me into their fold because I believe that change must be slow.'[35] This sums up a social philosophy which Marshall retains all through. The belief that change must be slow is reiterated in his later writings also. Reflecting on the 'possibilities of the future' more than three decades later, Marshall observes: 'There cannot be a great sudden improvement in man's condition of life; for he forms them as much as they form him, and he himself cannot change fast.'[36]

Marshall also, like Mill, speculated on the future of the working classes. Unlike Mill, however, the question that he raised is not how power would be transferred to the working class, but 'whether progress may not go on steadily if slowly, till the official distinction between working man and gentleman has passed away, till, by occupation at least, every man is a gentleman'.[37] His answer to the question is: 'it may, and it will'. And he relies for this accomplishment on innovations in the methods of production which would gradually, yet assuredly, accompany improvements in science and technology. These improvements, Marshall believed, would in the natural course diminish the need for disagreeable work and open up possibilities for an increasingly large section of the workers to lead a comfortable life. Spread of education, he argued, would hasten the process, enabling the working class increasingly to assimilate the training necessary for higher types of work. Marshall thus believed that there were possibilities, within the existing social order,

[33]A. Marshall, *Principles*, p. 335.
[34]Ibid., book VI, ch. IV, especially sect. 6.
[35]Quoted in *Early Economic Writings*, vol. 2, p. 351.
[36]*Industry and Trade*, 4th edn (Macmillan, London, 1923), p. 665.
[37]See paper on 'The Future of the Working Classes', *Memorials of Alfred Marshall*, p. 102.

of a gradual elimination of the causes of class conflict. In this he was clearly more optimistic than Mill.

Marshall was a defender of the capitalist system, even though he recognized its blemishes. His defence, however, has to do not so much with allocational efficiency as with technological efficiency. Here again he inclines rather towards the classics. His plea for freedom of industry and enterprise rests primarily on the fact that it stimulates individual initiative and creates an environment favourable for 'much subtle division of labour'. In Marshall's system, competition is not just a matter of numbers, it is essentially a matter of the extent to which one is afforded opportunity freely to use one's energy and resourcefulness in organizing production; Marshall identified competition with 'economic freedom'.

Viewed in this perspective, even monopoly is seen to have a beneficial aspect. The fact that some firms come on top suggests that they are run by men who have leadership qualities and can take advantage of economies of scale. Monopoly production is not thus necessarily against the interest of consumers. In the first place, the supply schedule of a commodity under monopoly is, from the nature of the case, lower than it would be if production were distributed among a large number of competing firms; the monopoly firm being larger in size enjoys larger economies of production. Secondly, it is not always that the monopolist is interested in his own net revenue only; it pays him to sell at a price lower than that which would maximize his immediate net revenue, in order that consumers might become familiar with his product. He may be led to maximize, not the monopoly net revenue, but an amalgam of the net revenue and the consumers' surplus associated with the sale of his product.[38] The consequent increase in sales would lead to further economies of production and hence to a further decline in costs. Altogether therefore monopoly price, it is argued, might turn out to be lower than it would be under perfectly competitive conditions.

Marshall had sympathy for the motivation of socialists, their concern for the poor and their passion for moulding society for the benefit of the people. But he was opposed to their method. He was aware of the limitations of the existing order – the inequalities of wealth and power that it tends to create. He would indeed favour

---

[38]Marshall calls this amalgam 'total benefit', or 'compromise benefit' according as consumers' surplus is equated fully with the monopoly net revenue or with a fraction of it. For all this, see A. Marshall, *Principles*, book V, ch. XIV, sects. 5 and 6.

a certain redistribution of property. But action on this, he would argue, should be limited to taxes and bounties. He had little faith in the public management of industries. 'The total remuneration that competition awards to men of business is probably less than would have been wasted without good to anybody if the same business had been done by Government. But wastefulness is the least evil of Government Management. A greater evil is that it deadens the self-reliant and inventive faculties, and makes progress slow. But the greatest evil is that it tends to undermine political, and through political, social morality.' This is what Marshall wrote in 1885.[39] It remained his abiding view. He believed in a spontaneous growth of the economy, urged on by the pecuniary motive of producers. Men being what he saw them to be, it remained his belief that progress depended upon 'the extent to which the strongest, and not merely the highest, forces of human nature' were brought into action for the furtherance of social good.[40]

[39]*Early Economic Writings*, vol. 2, p. 342.
[40]See A. Marshall, *Industry and Trade*, p. 664.

8

Keynesian Perspective

Background

'The *General Theory* has itself become classic – a work which the active theorist need not consult but in which historians of economic doctrines will have a lasting interest.' This is what one of the best-known interpreters of the economics of Keynes says, while introducing his subject.[1] It is as a classic, marking a distinct epoch, that Keynes's *General Theory of Employment, Interest and Money* finds a place here. The *General Theory* is indeed a classic, in a manner in which the *Wealth of Nations* is a classic. If Adam Smith by his *Wealth of Nations* laid the foundation of classical political economy, John Maynard Keynes by his *General Theory* has laid the foundation of a new system of economics, a system which is distinct not only from marginalist economics, as we have defined it, but also very significantly from classical political economy.

We have seen that the marginalists turned economic theory away from an analysis of the progress of aggregate wealth over time and its distribution among classes, and reduced it to an analysis of the problem of relative prices of individual commodities and factors under static conditions. Marginalism, we have argued, marked a fundamental departure from classical political economy. We have also seen that Marshall attempted a synthesis of the two systems by applying the marginal technique to an analysis of the movement of price and output over time, but that his analysis was confined to a single industry, where the condition of demand was supposed to be given from outside. It was obvious that piecing together 'partial equilibria' in respect of individual markets would not provide an

---

[1]Axel Leijonhufvud, *On Keynesian Economics and Economics of Keynes* (Oxford University Press, New York, 1968), p. 3.

121

answer to the problem of industry as a whole, if only because for industry as a whole demand could not be taken so readily to be given from outside.

Keynes asks a question which involves an analysis of the progress of industry as a whole. He asks if at all there exists a mechanism in the working of the capitalist system which guarantees a tendency to the full employment of resources of an economy. The marginalists bypassed the question by concentrating exclusively on allocation of given resources, while the classical economists took the tendency for granted, leaning on the hypothesis that for the economy as a whole demand is derived from the supply of commodities. They thus contended that growth does not have a limit except in so far as it is caused by scarcity of resources.[2] Adam Smith believed in the possibility of the continuance of a progressive state; if he ever thought, as he did indeed, of the possibility of a shrinking investment opportunity it was because, with growing prosperity, he expected labour to grow scarce relative to other resources and hence wages to rise. Ricardo, as we know, would attribute the possibility of a limit to growth to diminishing returns from land. Demand deficiency was ruled out by both. What is not consumed today would, they argued, be turned via accumulation into capital goods for the production of commodities which would be consumed tomorrow; the urge to accumulate on the part of the capitalists was supposed to be sufficient to ensure full employment of resources as a long-run tendency.

There was one dissenting note, however. It was from Robert Malthus, famous as the author of the theory of population. The classical economists, let us recall, posed much the same set of questions, but their answers differed. Here is one such question, the question as to whether demand could not be a constraint on productive activity. The long debate between Ricardo and Malthus on gluts remains one of the most exciting episodes in the history of economic theory – Malthus contending that the cause of falling profits lay in the deficiency of effective demand consequent on too rapid accumulation of capital, and Ricardo maintaining that it was all a question of diminishing returns from land and a consequent rise

---

[2]Keynes considers the marginalist theory of the allocation of given resources as being in the Ricardian tradition, thus arguing that Ricardo was concerned solely with the problem of prices of goods and services. See J. M. Keynes, *The General Theory of Employment, Interest and Money* (Macmillan, London, 1936), p. 4n. If, however, our interpretation of Ricardian economics is correct, then Keynes would seem to have misjudged Ricardo.

in wages. Malthus questions Say's law of markets (as it later came to be known), namely that 'supply creates its own demand'. According to this doctrine, which Ricardo accepted, effective demand for the economy as a whole could not be deficient in so far as the savings of the community were converted via investment into productive capital. Malthus, like Smith or Ricardo, defines accumulation as the conversion of savings from revenue into capital, and he agrees that for continued increase of wealth to take place in an economy accumulation is a necessary condition. Yet, he argues, accumulation can be too rapid for the products of industry to find a market at prices which would cover costs. Given that 'the capitalists, together with the landlords and other rich persons, agreed to be parsimonious, and by depriving themselves of their usual conveniences and luxuries to save from their revenue and to add to their capital', how is it possible, Malthus asks, 'that the increased quantity of commodities, obtained by the increased number of productive labourers, should find purchasers, without such a fall of price as would probably sink their value below costs of production?'[3] Elsewhere, in the same vein, he observes: 'under a rapid accumulation of capital, or more properly speaking, a rapid conversion of unproductive into productive labour, the demand, compared with the supply of material products, would prematurely fail, and the motive to further accumulation be checked, before it was checked by the exhaustion of the land'.[4]

Ricardo is left undisturbed. As his notes on Malthus's *Principles* show, he has no difficulty in arguing back that, on Malthus's supposition, wages of productive labourers would rise and demand would be sustained, although profits would tend to fall. Unproductive consumption is quickly dismissed as a wasteful method of maintaining the motive for accumulation; it is just as effective, Ricardo argues, as 'a fire which should consume in the manufacturers warehouse the goods which those unproductive labourers would consume'.[5] Malthus reiterated his views (repeating the same arguments, though) in a series of letters to his friend. But Ricardo remained unconvinced. Later economic theory absorbed the Ricardian doctrine; the theory of effective demand for which

[3]*Notes on Malthus's Principles of Political Economy*, reprinted in *The Works and Correspondence of David Ricardo* ed. P. Sraffa (Cambridge University Press, 1951), vol. II, p. 303.
[4]Ibid., p. 421.
[5]Ibid., p. 421.

Malthus fought went unheeded. Malthus remained the author of the *Essay on Population*; his *Principles* came nearly to be forgotten.

Keynes deplores the continued neglect of Malthus's line of approach, and in his *General Theory* he recognizes Malthus as his forerunner. However, where Malthus failed, Keynes succeeds. How does one explain this volte-face in the field of economic theory? To Keynes, Ricardo's 'victory' appears to be 'something of a curiosity and a mystery'. Curiosity, yes; but is it such a mystery after all? This is where our periodization assumes importance. Keynes writes more than a century after Malthus. The world that he faces could not be the same as the one into which Malthus projected his theory. In one of his letters to Ricardo, which may here be recalled, Malthus writes, apparently in desperation: 'We see in almost every part of the world vast powers of production which are not put into action, and I explain this by saying that from want of a proper distribution of the annual produce adequate motives are not furnished to continue production'.[6] To which Ricardo very aptly replies: 'I should not make a protest against an increase of consumption, as a remedy to the stagnation of trade, if I thought, as you do, that we are now suffering from too great savings . . . Such and such evils may exist, but the question is, do they exist now? I think not, none of the symptoms indicate that they do.'[7] The problem that perplexed Keynes so pressingly in the nineteen thirties – the problem of excess capacity and idle labour – could be dismissed by Ricardo in the eighteen twenties as non-existent! True, Malthus's formulation of the theory was weak, and Ricardo could easily pick holes in it.[8] But more than that, the message which he sought to convey was not appropriate for the economy to which it was addressed; the nineteenth century British economy was not ripe for a theory of insufficiency of effective demand.[9]

---

[6]Ibid., vol. IX, p. 10.

[7]Ibid., p. 26-7.

[8]Malthus relied for his theory on sheer intuition. Keynes recognized this. 'Malthus's defect', he notes, 'lay in overlooking entirely the part played by the rate of interest' (J. M. Keynes, *Essays in Biography* (Macmillan, London, 1933), p. 147). Yet he condones it. Keynes's biographer, R. F. Harrod, thinks, very rightly, that in this respect Keynes allows his generosity to be carried too far. 'He [Keynes] finds, for example, in Malthus a precursor of his own theory of "effective demand". I cannot believe that Malthus, splendid as he was as a population theorist, contributed much of value to economics, in which he was always muddled.' See R. F. Harrod, *The Life of John Maynard Keynes* (Macmillan, London, 1951), p. 460.

[9]Surely Keynes makes an extravagant claim for Malthus, as he lets himself say: 'If only Malthus, instead of Ricardo, had been the parent stem from which nineteenth century

If classical political economy was the product of the Industrial Revolution, Keynesian economics is the product of the depression of the thirties. A century and a half intervened between the two events. Formidable changes took place in the meantime in the structure of the economy which concerned Smith or Keynes. The depression came, as it were, as a signal pointing to these changes. Keynes realized that the depression could not be viewed as just a downswing of a business cycle, as orthodox economy theory would view it. It is significant that he characterizes the state which his system represents as unemployment *equilibrium*. The *General Theory* is the economics of secular depression – counterpart, as one may say, of a 'secular boom' that the British economy experienced in the wake of the industrial revolution.[10] The cycle is recognized; but it is supposed to move round a trend line which is itself depressed.

Method

The focus of the *General Theory* is on the short period, Marshall's short period. The quality and quantity of available equipment, the supply of specialized skill and ability and of supervision and

---

economics proceeded, what a much wiser and richer place the world would be today!' (J. M. Keynes, *Essays in Biography*, p. 144). To ask for the maintenance of a leisure class, as Malthus does, for the sake of unproductive consumption, is surely a dangerous counsel for a developing economy – and England, for the best part of the nineteenth century, *was* a developing economy. See what Keynes himself has to say about nineteenth-century Europe: 'The new rich of the nineteenth century were not brought up to large expenditures, and preferred the power which investment gave them to the pleasures of immediate consumption . . . Herein lay in fact, the main justification of the Capitalist System . . . If the rich had spent their new wealth on their own enjoyments the world would long ago have found such a regime intolerable. But like bees they saved and accumulated, not less to the advantage of the whole community because they themselves held narrower ends in prospect.' J. M. Keynes, *The Economic Consequences of the Peace* (Harcourt, Brace and Howe, New York, 1920), pp. 18–19.

[10]'One cannot repress the thought', observes J. R. Hicks, 'that perhaps the whole Industrial Revolution is nothing else but a vast secular boom.' J. R. Hicks, *Value and Capital* (Oxford University Press, London, 1939), p. 302n. If it is so, one could say also that the period between the two Great Wars, the period relevant to the *General Theory*, marks the beginning of a secular depression as a sequel to the boom.

At one time ('Mr Keynes and the Classics', *Econometrica*, 1937) Hicks defined the *General Theory* as the 'Economics of Depression'. Later he wished to withdraw it, saying that the definition would be misleading if it were taken in its usual meaning. See J. R. Hicks, *Economic Perspectives* (Oxford University Press, London, 1977), p. 84n. The definition here suggested, one hopes, will be found to be free from ambiguity.

organization, as also the technique of production are taken as given, just as in Marshall's short period. However, whereas Marshall's analysis is confined to a single industry and is directed to the determination of price in the market for a single commodity, Keynes's analysis is concerned with the entire economy and is designed to show how the aggregate volume of employment is determined.[11] Keynes's aggregate supply function and the aggregate demand function relate employment to 'proceeds' of the output of industry as a whole (or income, as it may also be called). Keynes has thus a problem of aggregation, even as the classical economists had, and he proposes what he calls 'wage-unit' (money wage of a unit of labour) as his measure for purposes of aggregation.[12]

Since the reference is to a short period and since the output from the current employment forms a stream flowing into the future, the proceeds which are related to employment are *expected* proceeds. Thus, looked at from the point of view of the entrepreneurs, the aggregate supply price of output from a given amount of employment is the amount of proceeds expected from its sale, which would just induce entrepreneurs to give that employment. It is indeed our familiar 'cost of production', being payments to factors of production, including normal profit.[13] The demand price likewise is the amount of proceeds which the entrepreneurs actually expect to derive from a given amount of employment. These relationships yield a pair of curves – the supply curve and the demand curve; the curves relate, let us remember, to output of industry as a whole,

[11]It seems important to stress that Keynes' *General Theory* is a theory of employment. If output comes in, as it does, it comes in as an associate of employment. Given the technology of production, one of course follows from the other, and Keynes does often refer to both employment and output. Yet employment remains his primary problem. The purpose of the *General Theory* is to enquire why the economy was failing to give full employment to labour. It was later, in the context of underdeveloped economies, that the level of output and its growth came to the forefront, as indeed it did once at the time of the classical economists.

[12]The family resemblance between Keynes's 'wage unit' and Smith's 'labour command measure' should not be missed. The need for aggregation – involvement, that is, in the demand and supply of the aggregate of commodities – is what distinguishes Keynes's economics from Walras's general equilibrium theory, which also deals with the economy as a whole. The *numeraire* in Walras's system is not a measure, it is just a common denominator used to ensure consistency in relative prices. See chapter 4, p. 41, footnote 6.

[13]Keynes, however, leaves out what he calls 'user cost' from both 'supply price' and 'income'. The 'user cost' of Keynes is another name for what Marx would call 'constant capital' – raw materials used and the wear and tear of machinery. Keynes's supply price thus stands for *net* national income, while Marx, as we know, is concerned with *gross* national income.

measured in wage unit. So long as the aggregate demand price exceeds the aggregate supply price, it pays the entrepreneurs to add to employment. The economy settles at a level of employment which is defined by the intersection of the two curves. The approach is clearly Marshallian; the position where the economy is supposed to settle down is the Marshallian short period equilibrium, extended to industry as a whole. The aggregate demand at the point of intersection of the curves is called by Keynes 'the effective demand'.[14] As in Marshall, the analysis is in terms of a process of adjustment of supply to demand.

The stock of resources with which the period starts is the result of past operations, and current operations depend upon expectations about the future. Current employment thus depends upon the existing stock of resources and expectations about the sale proceeds of the output which results from employment. If, as Hicks would say, the short period of Keynes or of Marshall is self-contained, the self-containedness is an expository device; the end-point of a short period may as well be seen as a 'disequilibrium' situation in relation to a long-run trend. Thus, although Keynes chooses one particular short period for analysis, the movement of the economy may be conceived as a string of successive short periods, each connected with the other.

Now, in Marshall's system, as we have seen, there is a tendency to a long period equilibrium, which is determinate. Expectations in Marshall's short period are based on current prices. And since the condition of demand is given and constant and since transactions at 'false' prices do not alter the character of buyers and sellers, 'false' prices are relied on to lead to the 'true' long period equilibrium price, with the supply fully adjusted to demand. The long period of Marshall is truly self-contained. There is no such long period in Keynes's system. The short periods are no doubt connected by way of net accumulation, but expectations in each short period are based on current experiences, and they do not add up to anything like a determinate long period equilibrium. Long period in Keynes's system is history.[15] For Keynes, short period is the real thing to investigate; he would not live for the morrow, nor would he have us do so either – 'in the long run we are all dead', he once declared.

---

[14]The term has some analogy with Adam Smith's 'effectual demand'. Both refer to positions of equilibrium.

[15]See J. M. Keynes, *General Theory*, p. 306.

What should be the shape of the short period curves? Keynes's definition of aggregate demand and supply functions points to integral demand and supply curves; Keynes relates *total* proceeds to employment. However, for our demonstration to be in line with the Marshallian procedure, we shall here use unit demand and supply curves, measuring *average* proceeds along the vertical axis. Marshall's short period supply price of output, it will be remembered, is necessarily upward-sloping; capital equipment being given and constant, increasing use of labour and other variable resources is supposed to give rise to diminishing returns. In Keynes's system there is, to start with, excess capacity in capital equipment and there is unemployed labour; over a range therefore there is constant return to scale; under the conditions which Keynes postulates this may indeed be the relevant range – the range within which equilibrium lies. The Keynesian supply curve is thus seen as horizontal over the range. On extreme assumptions, namely that resources are all homogeneous and that labourers are willing to accept the same wage rate till full employment is attained, it would remain horizontal over the entire range covering unemployment and would be vertical at the point of full employment. Keynes, however, does not rule out the possibility of the curve turning upward at near-full employment.[16]

The position of equilibrium depends upon the position of the demand curve. As already noted, Keynes allows the demand curve to intersect the supply curve. In Keynes's system, as in Marshall's, the demand curve is downward-sloping. Thus beyond the point of equilibrium it lies below the supply curve. Figure 6, drawn on Marshallian lines, describes the situation.

In the figure employment is measured along the horizontal axis, and amount of 'proceeds' per unit of employment is measured along the vertical axis. Full employment, let us suppose, is at F. The supply curve SS' is drawn parallel to the horizontal axis until it meets FF', at which point it becomes vertical. On the alternative assumption it is allowed to have an upward bend at T, showing diminishing return or perhaps a rise in the wage unit. The curve thus meets FF' at s, at which point it becomes vertical.[17] Let dd', the demand

---

[16]For an enumeration of the conditions under which the supply price may rise with rising effective demand, see J. M. Keynes, *General Theory*, pp. 295-303.

[17]The diagram is adapted from John Hicks, *Economic Perspectives* (pp. 82-3). Hicks assumes that the supply curve is asymptotic to FF', thus arguing that 'Full Employment is strictly out of reach', whatever the demand. This, he suggests, is 'the natural way to take

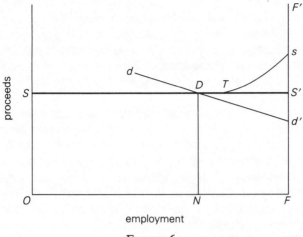

FIGURE 6

curve, intersect the supply curve at *D*. Draw *DN* perpendicular to the horizontal axis. The effective demand is at *D*, which, as shown in the figure, is to the left of *T*, and of course to the left of *FF'*. *NF* units of labour thus remain unemployed, even though unemployed labourers may be prepared to accept the market rate of wages, while their marginal product, if they were employed, would not be lower than the market wage; they are 'involuntarily' unemployed. With equilibrium at *D*, employment is *ON* and total income is *ONDS*. The economy is deprived of a possible output, which *NF* units of labour could produce had demand been sufficient.

Note that the demand curve is shown in the figure to be independent of the supply curve, as in Marshall's system. Now Marshall, as we have seen, assumes the demand to be given from *outside* the industry which happens to be his point of reference. Can the same procedure be used for industry as a whole? Is not aggregate supply the source from which aggregate demand is derived? What happens to Say's law of markets? Further why, even allowing demand to be independent of supply, should *D* lie necessarily to the left of *FF'*? These are the disturbing questions to which Keynes sought an answer. He knew these were live

___

it'. This is possible; but there seems to be no compelling reason for it. We have thus allowed our alternative supply curve to meet *FF'*. It will be our contention, on the other hand, that it is the property of the demand curve which Keynes highlights to show that equilibrium takes place at a point which is necessarily to the left of *FF'*, possibly to the left of *T*.

questions, for he found in his time that even a boom failed to carry the economy up to full employment level.[18] With the experience of the Great Depression behind him he turned to the behaviour of aggregate demand to explain why unemployment was tending to be a normal feature of the kind of economy in which he lived. He thus revives the old puzzle with which Malthus had wrestled unsuccessfully.

Analysis of the aggregate demand function forms the core of the *General Theory*. It is shown, first, that there are elements in the aggregate demand which are independent of the income (aggregate supply price of output, in other words) of the society, and, secondly, that the behaviour of these elements at a certain stage in the development of an economy is such as to prevent the full utilization of its resources. Limits to the growth of an economy, it is argued, are set by elements that govern the aggregate demand, as Malthus envisaged, and not by the scarcity of resources, as Ricardo would have it. The propositions of the *General Theory* are meant essentially to show how the demand constraint on growth assumes priority over resources constraint. We now turn to these propositions.

Propositions

Keynes splits up the aggregate demand for employment into two elements – demand arising from consumption, and demand arising from investment. Now, while consumption is a function of income, investment is not. In the classical system, including that of Malthus, there is no dichotomy between investment and saving; what is not consumed is supposed to be 'accumulated' towards the formation of capital. In the marginalist system, where the dichotomy is recognized, investment is supposed to be equated to saving via the rate of interest. In Keynes's system investment is autonomous in relation to income; the passage of the economy is from investment to income *and* saving, not from income to investment *via* saving. Investment, Keynes argues, is determined by the expected rate of return from an addition to the stock of capital ('marginal efficiency of capital', as he calls it) and the rate of interest, itself determined in the money market, independently of the level of income. An increment of investment produces a chain reaction on income

---

[18]See J. M. Keynes, *General Theory*, pp. 322–4.

working through what is known as the 'multiplier'; the resulting increment of income is such as to induce an increment of saving equal to the increment of investment. Saving, as well as income, is thus the result of investment, not its cause.[19]

Keynes thus dissociates the demand curve from the supply curve. The supply curve, as we have seen (figure 6), is horizontal over a range and then possibly upward-sloping. The demand curve, on the other hand, is shown to be downward-sloping, it being assumed that the marginal efficiency of capital declines with increasing investment and that the marginal propensity to consume declines with increasing income. Effective demand is thus shown to lie at the point of intersection of the two curves, much as in Marshall's partial equilibrium system.

But then, why should equilibrium lie inevitably to the left of FF', or perhaps on the horizontal range of the supply curve, as shown in our construction? As one answers this, one recognizes why the *General Theory* should be regarded as marking an epoch. 'During the nineteenth century' Keynes observes, 'the growth of population and invention, the opening up of new lands, the state of confidence and the frequency of war over the average of (say) each decade seem to have been sufficient, taken in conjunction with the propensity to consume, to establish a schedule of marginal efficiency of capital which allowed a reasonably satisfactory average level of employment . . . Today and *presumably for the future* the schedule of marginal efficiency of capital is, for a variety of reasons, much lower than it was in the nineteenth century.'[20] Herein is the essence of

---

[19]These relationships are by now familiar. Yet it would be well worth showing them explicitly. An increment of investment directly increases income by the amount of the investment. Out of the increment of income thus caused a certain proportion is consumed, the proportion depending upon the marginal propensity to consume. This additional consumption makes a further addition to income, which again causes consumption to increase in the proportion determined by the marginal propensity to consume. Thus the reaction continues until it exhausts itself, in so far as the marginal propensity to consume is less than unity. Increment of income is thus a multiple of the increment of investment. If the marginal propensity to consume is assumed to remain constant all along, the value of the multiplier can be derived straight from it. If k is the multiplier (to use Keynes's symbol), $\Delta Y = k\Delta I$, where ΔI is the increment of investment and ΔY is the resulting increment of income. Now k can be shown to be equal to $1/(1-c)$ (where c is the marginal propensity to consume) and hence to $1/s$ (where s is the marginal propensity to save). Thus $\Delta Y = (1/s)\Delta I$, or $\Delta Y/\Delta I = 1/s$ or $1/(\Delta S/\Delta Y)$, where ΔS is the increment of saving. Hence $\Delta Y/\Delta I = \Delta Y/\Delta S$, or $\Delta I = \Delta S$. Note that this is the end-point of a chain of reaction, a process of adjustment of income and saving to an act of investment, much as the formation of price in Marshall's short period is a process of adjustment of supply to demand.

[20]J. M. Keynes, *General Theory*, pp. 307–8 (my italics).

what the *General Theory* seeks to convey. Investment, which is the regulating factor in the determination of the level of employment, depends upon entrepreneurial expectations and these expectations – 'the schedule of marginal efficiency of capital' – depend, among other things, upon the capital stock that an economy has already accumulated as a result of past investments. On the other hand, what proportion of an increment of income the income earners on the average will be disposed to consume – 'the marginal propensity to consume' – depends, among other things, upon the level of income that the society has already attained. Where the capital stock has grown large relative to the labour force, the marginal efficiency of capital, other things remaining the same, tends to be low, while at the same time, as the level of income becomes large relative to population, the marginal propensity to consume tends to be low. Thus in an economy which has gone through a long period of accumulation and technological progress, the marginal efficiency of capital and the marginal propensity to consume may both be so low that, given the rate of interest, the urge to invest and to consume will not be sufficient to create an aggregate effective demand which would be consistent with full employment. In such an economy, equilibrium will necessarily be established at a point where there will be involuntary unemployment. There will no doubt be booms at times; a spurt of invention, for example, will stimulate entrepreneurial expectations and encourage investment. But the level that the economy has already attained may be so high that even a boom will not be strong enough to secure full employment; the economy, Keynes urges, will remain 'in a chronic condition of sub-normal activity'.

Would not, it will be asked, the persistence of unemployment in the economy result in a lowering of the wage rate? And would not a general fall in wages be a solvent of depression? The orthodox answer to the questions is clear; it is that the cure for unemployment – a natural cure – would be the tendency to a fall in wages consequent on a pressure in the labour market, unless the market encountered strong trade union resistance. Keynes is sceptical. Wage bargains, he argues, are in money, and while a general wage cut will reduce the cost of output, it will reduce prices also, short period prices depending primarily upon wages. Whether or not, therefore, a cut in money wage would succeed in reducing real wages is uncertain. Keynes's approach to the matter is different. In considering the implications of a general wage cut he brings in the ultimate determinants of employment and output – the marginal propensity to consume, the marginal efficiency of capital and the rate of interest.

Now, the effect of a general wage cut on the marginal propensity to consume is clear; it is unfavourable, in so far as the wage earners' marginal propensity to consume is higher than that of the profit earners. On the marginal efficiency of capital the effect is uncertain; it depends upon entrepreneurs' expectations concerning the future course of wage rates; it would be indeed unfavourable if the wage cut were expected to be followed by further cuts in the future, as may well be the case. As for interest, Keynes concedes that a fall in prices which results from a fall in wages might, in view of the emergence of surplus cash holding, reduce the rate of interest and thus stimulate investment. This, however, is a possibility only when the current rate of interest is at a level which permits downward flexibility. This, Keynes argues, is not at all a certainty. The decision not to spend does not necessarily mean a decision to buy bonds; it may mean a decision to go in for cash. When this happens, the wage cut fails to do the trick. Where entrepreneurial expectations are in a depressed state, the minimum feasible rate of interest may not be low enough to evoke an investment demand which would be adequate for full employment.

There is, however, one route by which a wage cut could conceivably stimulate investment. In an open economy a reduction in wages in one country, by lowering relative costs, would stimulate exports and thus increase foreign investment. This would happen, however, only if other countries did not retaliate. The world as a whole is a closed economy; it is as well, Keynes would say, that its constituents take cognizance of it.

Keynes does not work out the manner in which one short period is linked with the other; he does not give us a long-run theory of growth. The *General Theory*, however, provides enough hints to suggest the direction in which the economy would have a tendency to move, if left to itself. One can thus construct a trend line with reference to successive short periods, each carrying a legacy from its predecessor.

If one leaves out the vagaries of long-term expectations and also inventions that alter the technique of production, and if it is assumed that each short period ends up, due to current net investment, with a capital equipment which is larger than it started with, the trend line would surely appear progressively to recede from what may be called the 'full employment' growth path. Remember that the marginal efficiency of capital tends to be lower, other things remaining the same, as the capital stock becomes larger, and that the marginal propensity to consume tends to be lower, other things remaining the same, as the standard of living of the income earners becomes higher. It is thus inevitable that a capitalist economy, which depends for its productive activities solely on entrepreneurial expectations, should in its later stages of development experience a deficiency of effective demand as a constraint on employment. And once it falls into the under-employment trap, it continues in that state; indeed, as some economists would contend, it may do so till it finds itself in a position where net investment is zero.[21]

The situation is shown in figure 7. It will be noticed that the construction is similar to figure 5, which describes the progress of prices in Marshall's system. However, whereas in Marshall's case we assumed the reference line to be horizontal, showing a long-run state of stationariness, here our reference line must be upward-sloping. Since there is, as we assume, formation of additional capital in each period, our reference line has to be a 'full employment' growth line.

In figure 7 time t is measured along the horizontal axis (as in the Marshall case) and income is measured along the vertical axis

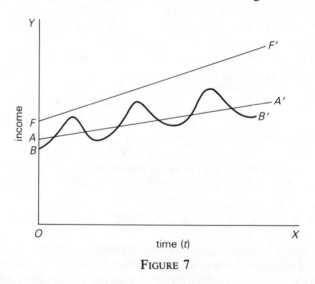

FIGURE 7

[21]See, e.g., M. Kalecki, 'The Marxian Equations of Reproduction and Modern Economics', in *Marx and Contemporary Scientific Thought* (Mouton, The Hague, 1969), pp. 319–20.

(corresponding to price in the Marshall case). *FF'* represents the 'full employment' growth path, and *AA'* represents the actual growth path. Vicissitudes in the form of booms and depressions are represented on the curve *BB'*.[22] *AA'* is shown progressively to be receding from *FF'*. This is just in conformity with the propositions of the *General Theory*. 'The richer the community', Keynes tells us, 'the wider will tend to be the gap between its actual and its potential production'.[23]

It should be noted that the line *AA'*, as drawn here, does not carry any suggestion of a norm; it only represents a succession of short period equilibria. The curve *BB'* represents booms and depressions arising, as Keynes suggests, from fluctuations in the marginal efficiency of capital; there is no concept of a 'normal level of employment' in Keynes's system. This indeed is where Keynes's trade cycle theory differs from the traditional theories. In the latter, depressions are supposed to be just displacements from the full employment path, to which the economy is supposed to have a persistent tendency to return; demand deficiency does not have a place there.

Marshall no doubt showed an awareness of the possibility of a hitch between the urge to save and the urge to invest. 'But though men have the power to purchase they may not choose to use it. For when confidence has been shaken by failures, capital cannot be got to start new companies or extend old ones. . . . There is but little occupation in any of the trades which make fixed capital. Other trades finding a poor market for their goods, produce less; they earn less, and therefore they buy less; the diminution of the demand for their wares makes them demand less of other trades'. This, however, is a description of the depression phase of a cycle; contrary to what one might be inclined to believe, there is no suggestion here that the economy might stay at the depression level.[24] For Marshall goes on to say: 'The chief cause of the evil is a want of confidence.

---

[22]The curve is so drawn as to show, as Keynes would have us do, not only that booms are short-lived while depressions are enduring, but also that even the peak of a boom does not touch the full-employment line.

[23]J. M. Keynes, *General Theory*, p. 31.

[24]Recalling the passage, Joan Robinson, for example, says: 'Here is the germ of the theory to account for crises and chronic stagnation with which Keynes exploded Marshall' ('Marx, Marshall and Keynes', in *Collected Economic Papers*, vol. 2 (Basil Blackwell, Oxford, 1960), p. 16. This seems to be an unwarranted conclusion; 'chronic stagnation' was never in Marshall's mind, as the full text would show – it could not have been indeed, considering the time when he wrote.

The greater part of it could be removed almost in an instant if confidence could return, touch all industries with his magic wand, and make them continue their production and their demand for the wares of the others . . . The trades which make fixed capital might have to wait a little longer; but they too would get employment when confidence had revived so far that those who had capital to invest had made up their minds how to invest it. Confidence by growing would cause itself to grow; credit would give increased means of purchase and thus prices would recover'.[25] Marshall overtly repudiates the demand deficiency doctrine. 'It is true', he says, 'that in times of depression the disorganization of consumption is a contributory cause to the continuance of the disorganization of credit and of production. But a remedy is not to be got by a study of consumption, as has been alleged by some hasty writers . . . the main study needed is that of the organization of production and credit.'[26] There is little doubt that Marshall also, like other trade cycle theorists of his time, would consider depressions to be just a passing phase, an aberration from the long-run tendency towards the full-employment path.

Keynes's short periods carry a different implication. Though formally Marshallian, they stand by themselves, each carrying a legacy of the past and each being moulded by expectations which its existing equipment would warrant. In Keynes's world the direction of successive short period equilibrium is not towards the full employment path but away from it.

Marx and Keynes

The capitalist system, as Keynes finds it, is flawed. It is flawed in that it fails to guarantee full employment of the available resources in the economy. Worse still, the failure becomes increasingly acute as capital accumulates and the economy grows. The behaviour of the determinants of the system, as shown in the *General Theory*, is such that every step that the economy takes towards development in one period creates difficulties for the next period. While capital accumulation and the consequent rise in the standard of living are

[25]The quotations are from Alfred Marshall, *Principles of Economics* (Variorum edn), vol. 1, pp. 710–12.
[26]Ibid., p. 712n.

marks of economic progress, they themselves ultimately turn out to be a 'drag on prosperity'. Comparing two equal communities, using the same technique of production but possessing different stocks of capital, Keynes observes that 'the community with the smaller stock of capital may be able for the time being to enjoy a higher standard of life than the community with a larger stock'. But then he adds: 'when the poorer community has caught up the rich – as, presumably, it eventually will – then both alike will suffer the fate of Midas'.[27] A paradoxical observation, no doubt, yet it follows inevitably from Keynes's theory of effective demand.

This, let us remember, is the kind of prognosis at which Marx also arrives, following his analysis of capitalist development. 'The accumulation of capital', Marx observes, 'is slowed down by the falling rate of profit, to hasten still more the accumulation of use-values, while this, in its turn, adds new momentum to accumulation. Capitalist production seeks continually to overcome these immanent barriers, but overcomes them only by means which again place these barriers in its way and on a formidable scale'.[28] The route that Marx takes is different; his approach is from the production side – similar, as we saw, to Ricardo's; Marx's culprit is the *investor*, as Keynes's is the *saver*.[29] Yet both Marx and Keynes see, in the process of capitalist development, an ultimate tendency to a falling rate of profit while wages remain constant, and both attribute depression and unemployment to the capitalists' endeavour to prevent this tendency.

There is indeed much in common between Keynes and Marx. Both seek to analyse the properties of a capitalist system – a system where accumulation (or investment, as one calls it now) – is what sets the economy in motion, and whose working is motivated by the capitalists' expectation of profit. Thus investment is autonomous.

[27]J. M. Keynes, *General Theory*, p. 219.
[28]Karl Marx, *Capital* (Foreign Language Publishing House, Moscow, 1959), vol. III, p. 245.
[29]Marx dismisses the demand deficiency doctrine as 'sheer tautology'. 'That commodities are unsaleable means only that no effective purchasers have been found for them . . . But if one were to attempt to give this tautology the semblance of a profounder justification by saying that the working-class receives too small a portion of its own product and the evil will be remedied as soon as it receives a larger share of it and its wages increase in consequence, one could only remark that crises are always prepared by precisely a period in which wages rise generally and the working-class actually gets a larger share of that part of the annual product which is intended for consumption' (ibid., vol. II, pp. 410–11). It is thus gratuitous on the part of Keynes to have listed Karl Marx as one of those who had kept alive the 'great puzzle of Effective Demand' (J. M. Keynes, *General Theory*, p. 32); it seems clear that demand deficiency does not play any part in Marx's theory of crisis.

In Marx's view accumulation is a passion with the capitalists. Similarly Keynes also claims that the urge to invest is governed by the capitalists' 'animal spirits'.[30]

Keynes was indeed more classical than he thought he was.[31] The question that he asks in his *General Theory* is a classical question, a question to which Marx also gave an answer. The classical answer, beginning from Ricardo, to the question as to what sets a limit to the progress of wealth in a capitalist economy is of course that, in the absence of an adequate flow of innovations, profits tend inevitably to fall with increasing accumulation. If, however, in explaining why profits have a tendency to fall, Marx, like Ricardo, refused to lend countenance to the theory of demand deficiency which Keynes adopts, it is because Marx's environment was yet an 'advancing' capitalism, not an 'advanced' capitalism of Keynes's experience. Ricardian 'minimum subsistence' theory of wages still held the field in Marx's time, to which, rightly or wrongly, Marx adhered. Keynes, on the other hand, experiences the full fruition of the trade union movement in his country, and he finds that the level of money wages, which results from a bargain between capitalists and labourers, tends to be too high, relative to prices, for normal profits to be maintained at anywhere near the full employment level. Instead of the capitalist exploiting labour, it is a case, as Keynes views it, of both being victims of an affluent society. If indeed the current level of real wages were to be at an absolute minimum, Keynes, like Marx, would surely dismiss the theory of involuntary unemployment. 'If', he concedes, 'it were true that the existing real wage is a minimum below which more labour than is now employed will not be forthcoming in any circumstances, involuntary unemployment, apart from frictional unemployment, would be non-existent'.[32] But to suppose this to be true, Keynes urges, 'would be absurd'. Keynes's world is one in which the

---

[30]See J. M. Keynes, *General Theory*, p. 161–2. Considering the state of marginal efficiency of capital in the modern economy, Keynes observes: 'If the animal spirits are dimmed and the spontaneous optimism falters, leaving us to depend on nothing but mathematical expectation, enterprise will fade and die.'

[31]It is remarkable that Keynes goes out of his way to give sanction to the Ricardian one-factor model. 'I sympathise with the pre-classical doctrine', he observes, while analysing the properties of capital, 'that everything is *produced* by *labour* aided by natural resources and the results of past labour' (J. M. Keynes, *General Theory*, p. 213). Note, however, Keynes's use of the term 'classical'.

[32]Ibid, p. 10. This, one imagines, is sufficient reason why Keynes should have understood Ricardo's opposition to Malthus's theory of gluts.

prevailing (real) wage rate is high enough socially to permit a downward revision.

Where, however, Keynes differs in a major way from Marx is in his social attitude. Marx believed in discontinuous jerks shifting social relations from one state to another. Capitalism, according to him, is just a stage in social evolution, and would die a natural death on account of the inner contradiction from which it suffered. Marx's endeavour was to hasten the process. Keynes, too, saw a contradiction in the system; but he sat down to seek out means to save it from possible destruction. Keynes's object in analysing the properties of capitalism was indeed to understand where it went wrong and what treatment it needed for its survival.

The measures that Keynes proposes for toning up production and employment have implications which socialists would welcome. Fiscal measures towards redistribution of income in favour of the relatively poor, direction of banking policy towards a gradual reduction in the rate of interest until it results in the 'euthanasia of the rentier', above all, direct intervention of the state in the sphere of investment – these are prescriptions which no doubt smack of socialism. Yet Keynes is not a socialist. Far from it. The sole purpose of his exercise is to fill in the lacuna in *laissez-faire* capitalism and to make capitalism acceptable to society. The task of the state here is to raise entrepreneurs' expectation of profit and to stimulate consumption, so as to keep up the level of effective demand.[33] Once this is assured, he would leave the economy to the play of capitalist forces. Keynes essentially is a believer in private initiative and free enterprise. For these, he holds, are the best safeguard not

---

[33]Keynes takes care to point out that spheres of state investment must not conflict with those of private investors. His plea for items like 'digging holes in the ground' is not to be taken as if it is just casual. It is meant to underline the condition that the investments that the state is supposed to undertake must not add to the stock of capital on which entrepreneurs' expectations are based. For if they did, the measure would clearly be self-frustrating.

It should be of interest to note that Keynesian involuntary unemployment is an example, a conspicuous example, of what Pigou describes as a discrepancy between marginal private net product and marginal social net product. Underemployment equilibrium is supposed to be a situation where an additional dose of investment, taken by itself, is not profitable, considering the expected 'private' net return, although, when its secondary repercussion on various consumption-goods industries – the so-called multiplier effect – is taken into account, the investment turns out to be socially profitable. Hence the need for state intervention. See on this A.K. Dasgupta, *Phases of Capitalism and Economic Theory and Other Essays* (Oxford University Press, Delhi, 1983), ch. 2, sect. II; also A. K. Dasgupta, *Planning and Economic Growth* (George Allen & Unwin, London, 1965), p. 31n.

only for productive efficiency but also for freedom of choice and the 'variety of life' to which it caters.

Keynes thus stands solidly in the British liberal tradition – in the tradition of Smith, Mill and Marshall. If his social prescriptions appear somewhat radical as compared with those of his predecessors, it must be remembered that he lived in an age which was radically different from the age in which his predecessors lived.

9

Overview

How It All Stands

We have taken a long journey, covering more than a century and a half of economic theory. We have made the journey quick, however, by concentrating on broad features of the various movements that have taken place in the field over the period. The period has been divided into three epochs and the contributions of representative economists have been considered in respect of each epoch. We have found that economic theory has grown round questions that have appeared to be significant in these epochs, thus exhibiting a certain discontinuity in its development. It has been indeed my endeavour to show that the propositions of economic theory, as we know them, operate within a limited field, limited to the specific relationships which they are intended to interpret. Our study has special reference to conditions in England. For it is in the context of British experience – the Industrial Revolution and its aftermath – that major developments in economic theory have taken place.

It will have been observed that the systems of economic theory that are associated with our three epochs are all conceived within the framework of capitalism. However, they belong to different phases of capitalism. Classical political economy grew when capitalism was in its early, vigorous phase, when labour had an entirely passive role in production and distribution, and when the more conspicuous happenings were accumulation and growth. Marginalism came when capitalism found itself in what may be called its placid phase. In spite of growing trade union assertion, the system held its own, being able to maintain a reasonably steady level of employment and output. Economists thus could afford to take a philosophic attitude to happenings around them and to concentrate on methodological issues, such as the viability of a decentralized system of production and exchange. The background of Keynesian economics is a decadent capitalism; having lost its original vigour and facing established trade unions in the labour market, the institution now needed a prop if it were to be sustained.

Our story began with Adam Smith and ended with John Maynard Keynes. Undoubtedly Smith and Keynes had a similar approach to economic theory. Both enquired into the factors that make for the prosperity of a nation, and both identified capitalist enterprise as the primary factor of growth. Both asked also if there were forces that might thwart the operation of these factors. Yet with all this they stand on different – one might say, opposite – poles. Smith was impressed by the spontaneity of accumulation and enterprise and found in prevailing state regulations an obstacle to the full realization of the outcome of the capitalist spirit. Keynes, on the other hand, found this spirit dimming and pleaded for state intervention as a means to stimulate it. The contrast between the two is seen conspicuously from their attitude to mercantilism. Clearly Smith's theory of division of labour was a challenge to the 'mercantile system' (as he would call it). On the other hand, it is just this system which Keynes was led, by his theory of effective demand, to rationalize. Smith's policy prescription was towards *laissez-faire*, Keynes's was away from it. The classical economists in general took the capitalist system for granted. Not of course Karl Marx. In the scheme of classification suggested here, Marx occupies a special position; while he had his feet firm on the classical ground, his gaze was on possibilities which Keynes was to explore, the possibilities of a crisis of capitalism.

Where do the marginalists stand? Viewed in the perspective of the above two systems – the perspective of the progress and decay of a national economy – marginalism would appear to be a kind of an interlude in the course of the development of economic theory. Influential as its theorems might be in their own context, marginalism was impervious to questions that provoked Smith, Marx or Keynes.

Relevance

If the view of the development of economic theory suggested here is correct, then it follows that a student of economics, unlike his counterpart in the natural sciences, can ill afford to ignore old theories just because they are old. Since, as we have found, systems of economic theory have grown historically in response to specific situations, each system has its relevance in appropriate contexts; an older theory may indeed turn out to be a more appropriate one in the context of an economy where conditions now are similar to those that had once evoked it.

I have already referred to the vicissitudes of the theory of wages. Classical economists could be content with a subsistence wage theory, writing at a time when labour was abundant. The Western economies have outlived this state; the minimum subsistence theory of wages is surely outmoded there. Yet there is a large part of the world where even today distress selling of labour is a common feature. In India, for example, even in the so-called 'formal' sector where there are trade unions to bargain in the labour market, one is not sure if the prevailing wage rate is at all above what, by any reasonable standard, one could recognize as minimum subsistence. Outside the formal sector conditions are much worse. In underdeveloped economies labour remains unemployed, not because wages are too high, but because they do not have enough capital to accommodate the existing supply even at a subsistence wage.

For such economies much of the Keynesian 'New Economics' would appear to be irrelevant, and some of Keynes's policy prescriptions would be positively harmful. Saving propensity would appear to be a virtue there, and unproductive consumption a vice. A transfer of wealth from the rich to the poor would of course be favoured; but it would be favoured, not as a measure to stimulate consumption, as Keynes would have it, but as a measure to raise efficiency and to stimulate productive effort. The constraints from which these economies suffer arise from a deficiency of resources which worried Ricardo, not from a deficiency of demand to which Keynes adapted his policy prescriptions. Keynes's theory of involuntary unemployment is clearly a special theory, conceived in the context of a mature capitalist economy; it fares badly when carried over to an economy which is just emerging from a feudal state.[1]

Nor is marginalist economics, as we have defined it, of much relevance to the less developed economies. The questions that are

[1] A situation where the aggregate demand curve intersects the aggregate supply curve within the horizontal range of the latter, or where the rate of interest settles within the horizontal range of the liquidity preference curve, is surely a special situation. A theory which represents such a situation, whatever it is, is not a 'general theory'.

paramount in the context of these economies relate to mass poverty and stagnation. They are questions to which marginalist economics, with its exclusive preoccupation with the principle of allocation of given resources, does not provide any answer.

For an answer to the sort of questions which would be of particular relevance to these economies one would have to look back to the classical economists. From Adam Smith one would learn how the extravagant spending of the landlord – 'a grandee in China or Indostan' – could result in the frittering away of the surplus that accrues to agriculture, or how the export surplus of a country would be of no avail if it were converted into precious metals and then 'buried'.[2] Ricardo and Malthus, with their newly discovered theory of rent, would show how there was a limit to land tax, trespass beyond which impaired not only the productivity of land but also the quality of the peasantry.[3] Similarly from Marx one would learn how, where the cultivator managed his own farm, 'the usurer may not only rob him of his entire surplus labour, but may also hack off a part of his wage'.[4] On the other hand, it is from these economists that one would get knowledge of the working of the growth-propelling forces in an economy – accumulation, invention and, above all, enterprise. Now this is the kind of economics in which the less developed countries of the world would find interest.

Writing in 1974, John Hicks remarked: 'The historian, for whom the second quarter of the twentieth century will be the age of

---

[2]See Adam Smith, *Wealth of Nations* (Everyman's Library, 1933) vol. I, p. 250. It appears that the same phenomenon is described in a more sophisticated manner by Keynes in the only passage in his *General Theory* which bears on India: 'The history of India at all times has provided an example of a country impoverished by a preference for liquidity amounting to so strong a passion that even an enormous and chronic influx of precious metals has been insufficient to bring down the rate of interest to a level which was compatible with the growth of real wealth' (J. M. Keynes, *The General Theory of Employment, Interest and Money* (Macmillan, London, 1936), p. 337). One could as well view the phenomenon, as Smith apparently did, as a simple case of substitution of precious metals for real capital. In any case the propensity is growth retarding.
[3]It may be of interest to note that Malthus's theory of rent owes its origin to his study of land revenue administration in India during his days at the Haileybury College. Malthus acknowledges it in the Preface to his *An Inquiry into the Nature and Progress of Rent* (John Murray, London, 1815). Malthus found the cause of economic stagnation of India in the fact that its 'sovereign' tended to appropriate for himself more than the 'net product' of land (which is rent, as he defines it), thus preventing a proper utilization of the land resources of the country.
[4]Karl Marx, *Capital* (Foreign Language Publishing House, Moscow, 1959), vol. III, p. 211.

Hitler, may well come to reckon the third quarter, now nearly completed, as the age of Keynes.'[5] Viewed from the side of the less developed part of the world, however, this latter period should rather be reckoned as the age of classical economists, especially of Karl Marx, considering the part which his 'extended reproduction scheme' has played in shaping plan models in the post-war period for what we now call 'developing economies'.[6]

[5]John Hicks, *The Crisis in Keynesian Economics* (Basil Blackwell, Oxford, 1974), p. 1.
[6]See, for an analysis of the relation of India's plan-model to Marx's extended reproduction scheme, A. K. Dasgupta, 'Marx's Reproduction Scheme and Indian Planning', in *Marx and Contemporary Scientific Thought* (Mouton, The Hague, 1969), pp. 346–50, reproduced in *Phases of Capitalism and Economic Theory* (Oxford University Press, Delhi, 1983), pp. 139–44.

Index